The Longman Guide to the Web

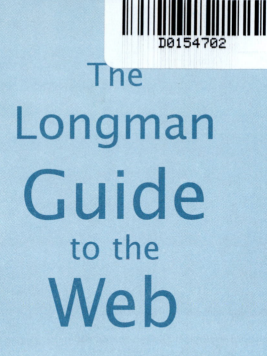

LESTER FAIGLEY

University of Texas at Austin

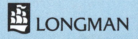 LONGMAN

An Imprint of Addison Wesley Longman, Inc.

New York • Reading, Massachusetts • Menlo Park, California
Harlow, England • Don Mills, Ontario • Sydney • Mexico City
Madrid • Amsterdam

Development Editor: David Munger,
                      The Davidson Group
Senior Development Editor: Sharon Balbos
Text and Cover Design: Wendy Fredericks
Cover Illustration: ©Wendy Grossman/Images.com
Project Manager: David Munger
Electronic Page Makeup: Susie Russum,
                        The Davidson Group
Senior Print Buyer: Hugh Crawford
Printer and Binder: The Maple-Vail
                      Book Manufacturing Group
Cover Printer: Coral Graphic Services, Inc.

The Longman Guide to the Web, by Lester Faigley

Please visit our Website at http://www.awlonline.com

ISBN: 0-321-06730-4

12345678910—DOC—02010099

Contents

Building a Multi-Page Site 85

Creating a Dynamic Site 97

Web Sites in the Disciplines 117

Doing Research on the Web 127

Using and Documenting Sources 147

What Else a Web Site Can Do for You   181

Appendix A: Glossary   193

Appendix B: HTML Tags   201

Preface

The growth of the Internet and especially the World Wide Web has impacted significantly on college courses; perhaps we've seen but a glimpse of what is soon to come when blazingly fast cable modem and ADSL connections give home users the kind of fast access enjoyed at college and corporate locations. Today many college courses have Web sites; indeed, some universities require them. *The Chronicle of Higher Education* (June 4, 1999) reports that "Some students say the best professors are the ones who bother to make Web pages for their courses. And a growing number of students use the quality of course Web pages as a decisive factor when picking classes." The Web has also become the medium of choice for research among many students who take advantage of universities placing reference collections, journals, and other resources online.

Instructors across the disciplines are requiring, or at least allowing, students to construct Web sites to fulfill assignments. Creating Web sites overcomes the problem of cross-platform incompatibility when using computers, and it encourages publishing for wider audiences—beyond the teacher and other students. Furthermore, publishing on the Web has become much easier. Web page editors remove the need to learn HTML, and the process of uploading files from a PC to an Internet server has also been greatly simplified.

The Longman Guide to the Web assumes that you will be expected to interact with course Web sites, and you will do research and publish work on the Web. It is designed to serve either as a primary text for those instructors who require students to create Web sites or as a supplementary text for instructors who do not devote class time to teaching Web publishing or online research skills but still expect Web competence. The explosive development of the Web often makes it seem chaotic. *The Longman Guide to the Web* offers a pathway through that chaos, giving you the knowledge you need to navigate the Web, design effective Web sites, and do research using the Web with ease.

Features of *The Longman Guide to the Web*

- **Straightforward presentation of how to publish and do research on the Web.** Concepts are presented in plain language, and basic tasks are set out in steps.
- **Presentation of research on the Web from a student's point of view.** Examples follow a student through the process of making a Web site and doing research on the Web.
- **Emphasis throughout on audience,** especially how to design a Web site that anticipates the needs of those who visit the site.
- **Instruction on documenting sources using MLA, APA, and COS styles.** Along with issues of intellectual property, special problems of online documentation are discussed.
- **Introduction to Web resources from across the disciplines,** including the humanities, social sciences, fine arts, business, and science.
- **Emphasis on Web design.** The nuts and bolts of HTML are increasingly hidden on Web page editors. The focus here is on sound design principles instead.
- **Instruction on using Netscape Composer,** a free Web page editor. Learning to use Composer prepares you for using more powerful editors that have additional functions.
- **Introduction to interactive uses of Web sites,** including forms, digital audio, animations, and digital video.

- **Instruction on how to write an effective online resume,** and other extracurricular uses of Web sites.
- **Companion Web site that offers additional examples and resources:**

  http://www.awlonline.com/researchcentral

Acknowledgements

I am grateful to my students and colleagues at the University of Texas who have taught me much of what appears in this book. In particular, I have learned a great deal from Peg Syverson and Sam Wilson, my brilliant colleagues in the Technology, Literacy, and Culture concentration. Sam and I team taught the first TLC course while I was writing this book, and he also reviewed the manuscript. Other reviewers who made helpful suggestions include: Robert D. Duval, West Virginia University; Susan Hines, La Salle University; Andrew Jones, University of California, Davis; Virginia Montecino, George Mason University; and Vicki Stieha, Northern Kentucky University;

I appreciate the work of others who contributed to this book, including Jon Camfield, whose expertise in interactive media provided the basis for Chapter 6. I greatly benefitted from a top-notch production team: Wendy Fredericks (text and cover design), Susie Russum (electronic page makeup), Jeanne Jones (copyediting), and Mike Shelton (proofreading). Sharon Balbos and Rebecca Gilpin at Longman supported the project in many ways from day one. Finally, I thank David Munger, who has been an outstanding editor in every respect and a delight to work with.

—LESTER FAIGLEY

The Digital Revolution

Imagine a communications technology so powerful that it radically changes how people conduct commerce and conceive of the world, even affecting what people understand as the time of day. Although you might think first of the Internet, earlier electronic technologies also had profound effects in the United States, beginning with the development of the telegraph in the 1840s. The telegraph changed the nature of newspapers, bringing the modern concept of a newspaper that carries late-breaking news. And because people were able to communicate with the speed of electricity through wires, they recognized the need for standard time zones. Before 1883, each town set its own time by determining exact noon—the point at which the sun was directly overhead. For example, when it was noon in New York City, it was 12:12 p.m. in Boston. In 1883, all the railroads in the United States and Canada adopted a plan for standard time zones, which the rest of the country followed in practice—and made official as law in 1918.

The impacts of technology

Each new electronic technology since the telegraph—telephones, phonographs, radio, television, fax machines, and a conglomerate of digital technologies—has had broad impacts on American life, impacts that for the most part their inventors could not have anticipated. Even though the Internet and the Web are but a few years old, they have become part of the daily lives of millions of Americans. Before 1991, few people who weren't connected to universities or the military had access to the Internet. And before 1994, even fewer were aware that the Web existed. For a new technology to become accepted so quickly suggests that people did not have to be convinced that they needed it. For those who had grown to depend on fast electronic technologies, being able to send and receive mail from people around the world in seconds, to shop online, to buy and sell stocks, to chat about nearly any subject imaginable, to have access to vast information resources, and to be entertained online seemed like the next step. Once people got hooked up, it felt like they had always been online.

The digital revolution unfolds

A remarkable combination of technologies makes up the Internet, but underlying all that you read, write, hear, record, draw, and watch on the Internet is a simple principle—that information can be stored and transmitted electronically in digital form. The basic unit of computing is a binary number or bit, represented as a 1 or 0. Bits can be combined into bytes that represent numbers, letters, and symbols. (A standard byte contains eight bits.) The principle, therefore, is as simple as an on-off switch, but the challenge was to build a machine that could manipulate thousands and eventually millions of switches. By 1951 the first commercial digital computers were available, which depended on vacuum tubes and occupied rooms the size of basketball courts. When transistor circuits replaced vacuum tubes in the 1960s and 1970s, computers rapidly became smaller, more reliable, and much more powerful. This process of miniaturization eventually led to microprocessor chips and personal computers, beginning with the Apple II, introduced in 1977, and the IBM PC in 1981. Users of personal computers discovered that they could do much more than calculate numbers. Personal computers made desktop publishing possible, giving writers opportunities to do things they were never able to do with typewriters such as change font types and rearrange the layout.

But it was not until the 1990s, when computers that could easily handle both graphical and textual information became affordable, that the digital revolution became a reality. Digital technologies have the potential to combine all previous electronic communications technologies into one big system, delivering television, movies, books, games, education, telephone service, shopping, business services, email, and a lot more on the same platform. Now the major holdup is not so much the computing power necessary as it is the bandwidth—the size of the pipe that delivers the Internet to your computer. As the bandwidth increases, you will be able to see and do more and more on the Web.

The Internet and the Web

For many people the Internet means the World Wide Web. There is a great deal more to the Internet than the Web, however, and the Internet has been around quite a bit longer. You may have heard that the Internet was originally run by the military. In fact, an early form of the Internet—the ARPANET—was developed in the 1960s by the U.S. Department of Defense in an effort to build an information network that could withstand nuclear war.

In 1969, the first files were transferred between UCLA and the Stanford Research Institute, and by 1971, the possibility of email became a research goal. But it took another development to make the Internet the leading force of the digital revolution. In 1990, Tim Berners-Lee and other scientists working at CERN, the European Laboratory for Particle Physics in Geneva, Switzerland, invented the Web. Their goal was to make possible the sharing of scientific papers, so at first the Web was a no-frills medium. In 1993, the first browser to gain widespread use—Mosaic—was developed at the University of Illinois, Urbana-Champaign, by Marc Andreessen and other students. Mosaic soon gave way to more advanced browsers—Andreessen's Netscape Navigator and Microsoft's Internet Explorer, which now battle for dominance in courtrooms and living rooms across America.

By 1996, nearly every college, institution, corporation, and government organization had a Web site, and they've been adding on ever since. We may have seen only a glimpse so far of what the Web will become. It's a revolution in progress that will change much of what you do in your lifetime. You can become an important player in the revolution.

Web Basics

Getting Started: Computers, Connections, and Browsers

Using public computers

Most colleges and universities today make it very easy for you to get started on the Internet. Often an account has been created for you when you register, and all you have to do is go to a computer lab, get the directions for logging in, give yourself an email name, and you're set to go. Just click on the Netscape or Internet Explorer icon.

Using your own computer

If you are in a dormitory room or apartment with an Internet connection, you will need a computer with a network card. Many newer computers already have the network card. If you have a computer without a network card, find out exactly which card you need and get it installed. And if you are shopping for a computer, find out what your particular college or department recommends and if any educational discounts are available. Your old computer

5

might work, but the browser and the software you'll need for multimedia take up big chunks of memory. Ideally, you should have at least 64 MB (megabytes) of RAM (random access memory) and a 4 GB (gigabyte) hard drive.

The big advantage of connecting to the Web directly from a computer lab or a building wired for the Internet is speed. Having a fast line doesn't matter that much for email but it makes a huge difference for the Web. Without a direct Internet connection, the process becomes more complicated and expensive and the results can be excruciatingly slow—especially if you want to hear and see the sounds, graphics, and video on the Web. You have two basic options: connecting by the slower dial-up modem or connecting through faster services offered by cable television companies (cable modems), by telephone companies (asymmetrical digital subscriber lines, or ADSL), or by satellite.

Installing a modem

Most people who connect to the Web from home use a dial-up modem. There are two kinds of dial-up modems: internal (built into the computer) and external (which you hook up). Internal modems are cheaper, especially if they are already installed. (Otherwise, you have to take the back off your computer and install the modem yourself.) Internal modems make things a little simpler, but they also draw on your computer's power supply and create extra heat. External modems must be connected to your computer and have their own power supply, so with the extra wires expect the wall behind your computer to look like a plate of spaghetti. Internal or external, you want the fastest modem you can afford. The minimum is a 28,800 bits per second modem (28.8 kilobits per second or 28.8 kbps) to see the images on the Web, and it still takes forever for the big ones to appear. If you have a slower modem, it's best to turn the images off. The standard modem is now 56 kbps, but often phone lines don't allow connections at full speed. In many locations you can now connect to the Internet through cable modem service offered by your cable TV provider or by ADSL offered by your phone company. These technologies are likely to be the way of the future because they provide high speed access that in theory runs up to 25 million bits per second (25 megabits or 25 mbps), but the usual range is between 384 kbps to 6 mbps. At this time cable modem and ADSL access to the Internet are quite a bit more expensive than dial-up modem connections. Wireless satellite connections are also available in some locations.

Connecting a modem

Most colleges now have dial-up connections to the campus computer network, and usually this option is cheaper than going with an Internet Service Provider (ISP) like America Online (AOL). When you connect your computer through your college network, you will probably have to go to the campus computer center to pick up a CD with the software you need. If you connect through an ISP, you'll also need some connection software supplied on a CD. (AOL and other ISPs mail out these CDs.) Either way, you pop in the CD and follow directions for configuring your system.

Using a browser

Finally, if you're using your own computer, you need a browser. Browsers are designed to read and display Web pages. Internet Explorer and Netscape Navigator are both free and one or both are likely included on the connection software CD you get from your school or ISP. If you are running Windows 98, Internet Explorer is already installed. Since you can download the latest versions of your browser for free, it's a good idea to get the current version. Just go to either Web site (http://www.microsoft .com/ie/ or http://www.netscape.com) and see if the version available there (numbered 4.1, 4.2, and so on) is higher than the version on your computer. Be advised, though, if you are downloading by a dial-up modem, it may take hours. You may want to get the update on CD from your campus computer center.

Other software you may need

When you download a browser, you also get a set of **plug-ins.** Plug-ins are separate programs designed to work with your browser. When you download Netscape, you get RealPlayer, QuickTime, LiveAudio, and Shockwave Flash among others. These plug-ins allow you to visit multimedia sites and to view video and hear music and sports broadcasts on the Internet. On Netscape, you can find out what plug-ins you have by opening the Help menu and going to About Plug-ins. When you don't have the right plug-in, you'll see a broken image and where to get the plug-in you need. Windows 98 and Windows NT versions of both Netscape and Internet Explorer have Active X, which gets the plug-in you need and automatically installs it. The only downside of plug-ins is that they take up a lot of memory and space on your hard disk. If your computer is marginal on memory and disk space, delete any plug-ins that you are not using.

Your home page

On your browser, "home page" means the page that appears when you start your browser. You can set your home page to whatever site you like; you don't have to use the page selected for you by your browser or ISP. Your school's main page is a good choice because it links to libraries, colleges and departments, catalogs and course schedules, upcoming events, and other important campus information. You can always return to this page quickly by clicking on "home" or the house icon on Netscape and Internet Explorer.

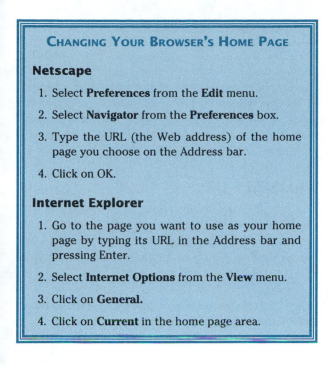

CHANGING YOUR BROWSER'S HOME PAGE

Netscape

1. Select **Preferences** from the **Edit** menu.

2. Select **Navigator** from the **Preferences** box.

3. Type the URL (the Web address) of the home page you choose on the Address bar.

4. Click on OK.

Internet Explorer

1. Go to the page you want to use as your home page by typing its URL in the Address bar and pressing Enter.

2. Select **Internet Options** from the **View** menu.

3. Click on **General.**

4. Click on **Current** in the home page area.

URLs

How can your browser pull up so much so quickly from around the world? The secret lies in the Web's system of addresses. The Web is a vast collection of files stored on millions of computers around the world connected by the Internet. Computers that are set up as Web **servers** organize the files that make up Web pages in directories. Each Web page has a specific address which appears in the Address bar at the top of a Web page.

The name of a Web page address is the **URL** (Uniform Resource Locator). You can type in a URL on the Address bar of your browser, but more often you make these connections through links—by clicking on words that are underlined or highlighted with a different color or by clicking on a graphic or button. Sometimes the link isn't signaled by a different color or underlining, but you can always tell if it's a link because the pointer turns into a pointing finger icon [☞] when it's over a link. Clicking on a link activates a URL, which your browser attempts to access. When you first use the Web, you may not pay much attention to the URLs, but later you will realize they are just as important as knowing phone numbers and street addresses.

What's in a URL

You can find out much about a Web site from its URL. If you are doing research on recent volcanic activity on Mount St. Helens in Washington, and you use a search engine, you might get this URL on your list:

http://vulcan.wr.usgs.gov/MSH/CurrentActivity/ 1999/summary_feb99.html.

PROTOCOL	HOST NAME	FILE PATH
http://	vulcan.wr.usgs.gov	MSH/CurrentActivity/ 1999/summary_feb99.html

These long addresses have three parts.

First, they begin with the **protocol,** which tells the browser what kind of page to look for. Most Web pages begin with **http://**, which is an acronym for Hypertext Transfer Protocol. Your browser can also access files that are not Web pages, which begin with **ftp://** or **gopher://** or other abbreviations.

Next, URLs include the **host name**—the address of the server where the page is located. The server address contains important clues about who owns the Web site. Working backwards on **vulcan.wr.usgs.gov**, we know immediately from the last part—called the domain name—that the site is government owned. The domain name tells you what kind of organization sponsors the site: **.com** (commercial), **.edu** (education), **.gov** (government), **.mil** (military), **.net** (commercial), and **.org** (nonprofit organization). Web sites outside the United States have codes for different countries such as **.au** (Australia), **.ca** (Canada), **.de** (Germany), **.fr** (France), **.hk** (Hong Kong), **.jp** (Japan), **.mx** (Mexico), and **.uk** (United Kingdom). The rest of the address tells us the name of the computer, **vulcan,** and the sponsoring organization, **usgs**—the United States Geological Survey.

The third part of the URL is a **file path** (**MSH/ CurrentActivity/1999/summary_feb99.html**) which allows the browser to find a particular Web page on a Web server. Files on a Web server are placed in folders just like on personal computers, which you'll learn more about in the next chapter. When your browser connects with the USGS Vulcan server, it looks inside the folder **MSH** for the folder **CurrentActivity,** and inside **CurrentActivity** for the folder **1999**. Then it looks inside **1999** for the file named **summary_feb99.html**. It is important to know how a URL address works because search tools on the Web often take you deep down in a Web site, and sometimes you have to work upwards by removing parts of the URL to figure out who put up the page. Another thing to remember about the path segment of a URL is that many servers are **case sensitive**, meaning that the browser distinguishes between upper and lower case. Thus, a browser will not find **summary_feb99.html** if you type **summary _Feb99.html**.

Root URLs

Some URLs do not have a file path and look like this: **http://vulcan.wr.usgs.gov/**. A URL without a file path is called a **root URL.** This URL takes you to the main page of the USGS Cascades Volcano Observatory. This main page of a Web site is also called the "index page" or the "home page" (a different meaning of "home page" than the first page you see on your browser). Most major corporations have a root URL, which is usually www.[NAME OF

COMPANY].com. Your browser will fill in a root URL for you, so, for example, if you type **gap** on the Address bar, the browser will pull up The Gap Online Store. Your browser also fills in http:// for you, so you never have to type it on the Address bar. Internet Explorer has a feature called Auto-Complete that completes the address while you type.

Browser Tools

Both Netscape and Internet Explorer offer some useful tools for doing research, publishing on the Web, and just cruising around. They are remarkably sophisticated programs that do much more than just display Web pages. On the menu bars of Netscape and Internet Explorer, you'll find tools that allow you to keep track of where you've visited in a browsing session, make lists of sites that you want to return to, save pages and graphics, and do several kinds of searches. Both Netscape and Internet Explorer also have email programs and other functions, which you may or may not want to use.

Netscape Tools

Netscape's tools are arranged on the top menu bar, with pull-down menus under each word, and on the Netscape bar below. The most powerful tools are in the pull-down menus (see Figure 1.1).

Keeping track of where you've been is a problem when you start clicking away on links. You can always work backwards using the back arrow on the Netscape bar. But a quicker way is to open the **Go** menu, which lists where you've been (see Figure 1.2). You can select the page you want to revisit.

Bookmarks are handy for keeping track of sites that you want to return to later. You can add any page to your bookmarks list simply by opening the **Bookmarks** menu and choosing **Add Bookmark.** If you keep adding pages (or sites), soon you'll have a long list that makes it hard to find what you want to

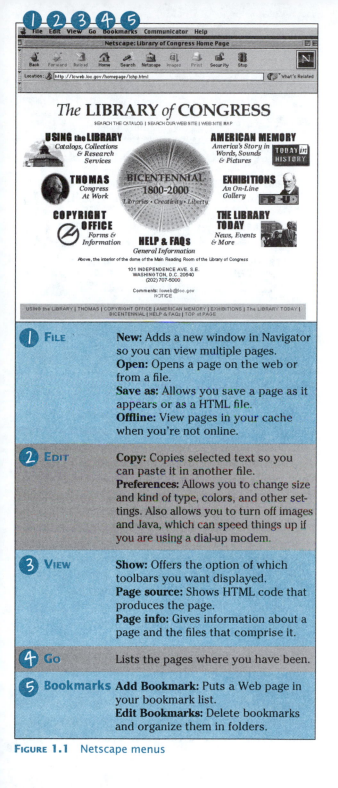

FIGURE 1.1 Netscape menus

FIGURE 1.2 Netscape's Go menu

go back to see. At this point you should organize your bookmarks into folders (see Figure 1.3). Open the **Bookmarks** menu and select **Edit Bookmarks.** You'll see a list of your bookmarks. Then open the **File** menu and select **New Folder.** You can then name the folder and drag the bookmarks into it. You can also save your bookmark file on a disk by using the **Save As** command on the **File** menu. Then you can take your bookmarks with you and use them on more than one computer. It's very handy if you do some of your work in a campus computer lab and some at home. You also can have more than one list of bookmarks, but you can see only one list at a time.

Many times you will see something on a Web page that you want to copy. If you only want some of the text on a page, it's easy to select the text, copy it using the copy command on the Edit menu, open a window on your word processing program, and paste in the text. You can also save an entire page

Name	Address	Date of Last Visit
▽ 📑 Bookmarks for Joe User		
▶ 📁 Search		
▶ 📁 Books		
▶ 📁 Courses		
▶ 📁 Health		
▶ 📁 Multimedia		
▽ 📁 Museums		
📄 WWW Virtual Library : Museums around...	http://palimpsest.stanf...	7/1/97 11:58 AM
📄 SILS Art Image Browser : Browse by M...	http://www.sils.umich...	6/28/97 6:22 PM
📄 museums and organizations	http://www.si.edu/org...	5/28/97 4:10 PM
📄 WWW Virtual Library : Museums in the ...	http://www.museumca...	6/28/97 6:05 PM
📄 WWW Virtual Library : Museums around...	http://palimpsest.stanf...	7/1/97 11:39 AM
📄 Library of Congress Exhibitions	http://lcweb.loc.gov/e...	5/22/97 1:01 PM
📄 United States Holocaust Memorial Muse...	http://www.ushmm.org...	4/3/97 4:06 PM
📄 WebMuseum : Famous Paintings exhibition	http://watt.emf.net/w...	6/12/97 2:52 PM
📄 The Art Institute of Chicago	http://www.artic.edu/...	2/23/98 11:32 AM
▶ 📁 People		
▶ 📁 Periodicals		
▶ 📁 Travel		
▶ 📁 Weather		

FIGURE 1.3   Bookmark folders in Netscape

using the **Save As** command, either as text or as an HTML file. You also can save images on the Web by right clicking on an image in windows or holding down the mouse button on a Mac to get a pop-up menu. On the pop-up menu select the **Save Image As** command. And you can print a page simply by clicking on **Print** or the printer icon.

When you click on **Search,** you are connected to Netscape Netcenter, which has a search engine and links to other search engines including Excite, Infoseek, Lycos, Snap, and LookSmart. Excite, Lycos, AltaVista, and Yahoo began as Internet search engines, but now have a great deal more on their sites, including news, maps, and special functions like People Finder. These one-stop Web sites are called **portals.** Each search engine is a little different, so try out several and compare the results for the same search. Knowing which search engine to use and how to narrow down a search are crucial for getting the results you want, which you'll find out more about in Chapter 8.

There are a few other things you should know about Netscape. Open the **Edit** menu and then open **Preferences,** where you'll find many options. You can change the size and kind of fonts displayed on the page. If the type is too little, you can make it bigger; if you want to see more of a page, you can make the type smaller. You can change the colors of links. You can add character sets if you are viewing pages in foreign languages. And if you are using a dial-up modem and getting frustrated because the pages are taking so long to load, you can also turn off the image files and disable Java and JavaScript. You'll miss the graphics, but at least you'll get to see the text.

Browsers don't download every page every time. Pages that you consult frequently are stored in a **cache.** The cache allows you to do some browsing when you are offline. It also speeds up the loading of pages. One thing to remember though is that the browser will look in the cache first. When you click on **Reload,** the browser will try to reload the file that is in your cache. Hold down the Shift key on Windows or the Option key on a Mac and click **Reload** to get the page from the Web. When you start putting up your own pages on the Web, remember how to get the page off the Web and not out of your cache.

Internet Explorer Tools

Like Netscape, the tools on Internet Explorer are arranged on the top menu bar with pull-down menus, but the terms are a little different (see Figure 1.4). For example, Explorer uses **Refresh** instead of Reload. Also, the links you save in Explorer are called **Favorites** instead of Bookmarks. You can organize your favorite sites in folders by clicking on **New Folder** in the Favorites menu. If you click on **Open Favorites,** you can rearrange and delete folders and files, and you can save your favorite sites on a disk file so you have them with you if you use more than one computer to connect to the Web.

The Explorer bar allows you to show a list of links on the left side of your screen while the page displays on the right side. For example, if you click the

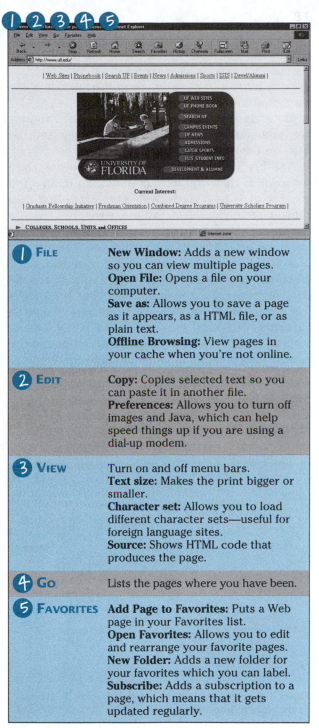

1 FILE		**New Window:** Adds a new window so you can view multiple pages. **Open File:** Opens a file on your computer. **Save as:** Allows you to save a page as it appears, as a HTML file, or as plain text. **Offline Browsing:** View pages in your cache when you're not online.
2 EDIT		**Copy:** Copies selected text so you can paste it in another file. **Preferences:** Allows you to turn off images and Java, which can help speed things up if you are using a dial-up modem.
3 VIEW		Turn on and off menu bars. **Text size:** Makes the print bigger or smaller. **Character set:** Allows you to load different character sets—useful for foreign language sites. **Source:** Shows HTML code that produces the page.
4 GO		Lists the pages where you have been.
5 FAVORITES		**Add Page to Favorites:** Puts a Web page in your Favorites list. **Open Favorites:** Allows you to edit and rearrange your favorite pages. **New Folder:** Adds a new folder for your favorites which you can label. **Subscribe:** Adds a subscription to a page, which means that it gets updated regularly.

FIGURE 1.4 Internet Explorer menus

History button, you'll get a list of the sites you've visited in previous days and weeks, organized in folders. When you click on one of the links, it is displayed on the right side (see Figure 1.5).

Similarly, when you select **Search** on the Explorer bar, you see the search engine on the left and the page on the right (see Figure 1.6).

Another difference between Explorer and Netscape is that Explorer allows you to update the content of your favorite Web sites according to a schedule that you select. Explorer either notifies you that there is new content or automatically downloads the new content, even when you aren't there. This feature is called **subscribe,** but unlike some Web sites where you actually have to pay to see the content, subscribing to a site with your browser is free. You'll find the **Subscribe** command on the **Favorites** menu, and you can see what you have subscribed to by clicking **Manage Subscriptions.** If the content is updated on a schedule set by the Web site owner, it is called a **channel.**

Like Netscape, Explorer allows you to select and copy text from a Web page and paste it into another file, letting you take notes as you browse. You can

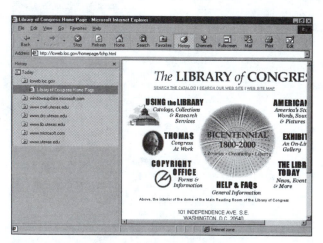

FIGURE 1.5 History of sites visited with page displayed on the right in Internet Explorer

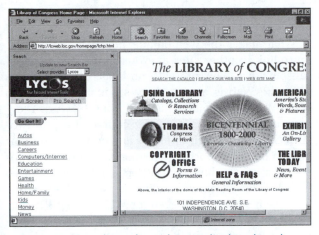

FIGURE 1.6   Search results with page displayed on the right in Internet Explorer

save entire pages with the **Save As** command, either as text or as an HTML file. You also can save images from the Web by clicking the right mouse button (Windows) or holding down the mouse button (Macintosh) until a pop-up menu appears. On the popup menu select **Download Image to Disk.** And like Netscape, Explorer stores the files you have recently visited in a cache and gives you the option of **Offline Browsing** (under the File menu). This option is useful if you are working with a dial-up modem and don't want to tie up your telephone line.

Why Make a Web Site?

If you have spent some time browsing on the Web but have never created a Web site, why should you take the time to learn how? First, the Web is the most powerful publishing technology ever created. If you have content, it doesn't take long to put up a bare bones Web site. With more effort, you can create a handsome site that many people will want to visit. You have an opportunity to let many people view your work and to communicate with other people near and far. It's not unusual to have people from other countries send you email when you put your site online.

What makes the Web unique, however, is the ability to link to other sites anywhere on the Web. You can put up a Web site with no links, but that's not what the Web is about. Many students create personal Web sites, which include links to work they have done for courses, to the course sites, and to sites concerning their interests and hobbies. You can make a personal portfolio of your work for others to see and create links for others to follow. People spend a lot of time building personal Web sites because it's useful, but even more because it's fun.

Once you get started, you'll want to learn more and create more ambitious Web sites. Most of the technical difficulties of making a Web site can be overcome quickly. The challenge is finding the best way to merge the content and design you want to present and the experiences you want visitors to have. Even though there are millions of pages already on the Web, the Web is still a very new technology, and you are among the generation of pioneers.

Steps in Creating a Web Site

The Technical Side

CHAPTER 2

Becoming a Web Publisher

Getting space on a Web server

If you have a computer and a connection to the Internet, you have most of what you need to become a Web publisher. The missing ingredient is the capability to share the pages you create with people around the world connected to the Web. You gain that capability by putting your pages on a Web server. Most colleges and universities allow students to publish Web pages on servers designated for student use. Before you can publish your Web page, you will need to set up an account and find out how to make your own subdirectory.

Probably your easiest option is to use a server at your college. Your computer center will have step-by-step directions on how to set up your subdirectory, and often these directions are posted on your school's main Web site under "computers" or "computing." Other options for publishing on the Web include:

1. Internet Service Providers such as AOL, CompuServe, Microsoft Network, Netcom, and Road Runner.
2. "Free" space offered on sites such as Fortune City (http://www.fortunecity.com), GeoCities (http://www.geocities.com), The Globe (http://www.theglobe.com), and Tripod (http://www.tripod.com). The catch about the "free" space is that you have to put up with a lot of advertising.
3. Your own computer as a Web server (which is considerably more advanced).

Get your space on a server first because you'll want to see your pages on the Web once you create them. Write down the Web address of the server, your login name, and your password. You'll need them when you put your pages on the Web.

Composing a Web page

To compose a Web page, you must learn how to generate HTML files. Although HTML looks complicated at first, it's a relatively simple computer language. You can compose Web pages in three ways:

1. With an **editor,** such as Netscape Composer, Microsoft Front Page, Claris Home Page, Macromedia Dreamweaver, or Adobe PageMill;
2. With a **translator,** such as Microsoft Word, Excel, or PowerPoint, which all have a "Save as HTML" command; or,
3. By **hand coding** HTML with NotePad on Windows, SimpleText on the Mac, or any word processing program.

Editors and translators do not require you to learn any HTML commands, but it's still handy to know a little about HTML. Sometimes the editor doesn't produce exactly the results you want, and you can open the source file, identify the problem, and fix it.

Using an Editor

Web page editors work like word processors, allowing you to add and edit text, but they also do a great deal more. On all editors you can add images and make links to other Web pages; the more advanced ones allow you to do things like create interactive questionnaires and incorporate the new enhancements to Web pages like Shockwave, RealMedia, and JavaScript.

Let's keep it simple and cheap for now. You can get Netscape Composer for free as part of the Netscape Communicator package (download the most recent version from http://www.netscape .com). Other editors have additional features, but all include the basic elements of Netscape Composer. Composer is a good program for a beginning Web designer. When you become proficient in Composer, you may want to move up to an advanced editor such as Macromedia Dreamweaver.

CREATING A BLANK WEB PAGE WITH COMPOSER

1. Start Netscape.

2. Select **New** from the **File** menu and then choose **Blank Page** (see Figure 2.1). You will see a Composer window.

3. Save your page by selecting **Save** command from the File menu.

4. Name your file **index.html** and click on **OK.** You will see the name of the file above the toolbars.

Working in Composer

To see what your page will look like when you put it on the Web, select **Browse Page** from the **File** menu. The Composer window remains open behind the Navigator window, and you can go back and forth as you make your page to see how it will look once it's on the Web.

The toolbars have icons for various functions which are quite similar to those of a word processing program (see Figure 2.1). You can find out what each does by moving the mouse pointer over the tool icon without clicking.

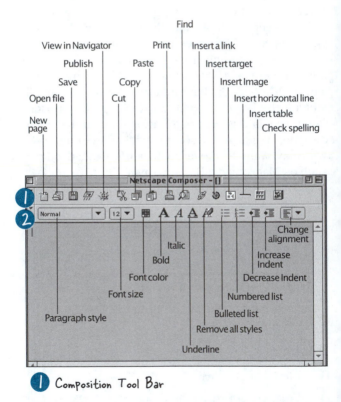

① Composition Tool Bar

② Formatting Tool Bar

FIGURE 2.1 Blank page in Composer

Now take a look at a student's home page as an example (see Figure 2.2). Rachel Jones introduces herself and then she tells about going on a sea kayaking trip in Alaska.

Rachel takes advantage of the possibilities to make links to other pages. She starts off by making links to her university and to her department by highlighting the words and then clicking the Link button:

The Link button pulls up the Link Dialog Box (see Figure 2.3), where Rachel types in the URL of the biochemistry department.

Rachel also wants to make some links to Alaska, and Composer makes this process extremely simple. To make a link to the Glacier Bay National Park Web site, she can highlight a link on the National Park Service directory, then drag and drop it on her page (see Figure 2.4).

She doesn't have to type anything, and you don't either if you can find an existing link to a site you want to link to.

![Screenshot of Netscape Composer showing Rachel's home page]

My Home Page

Hi. My name is Rachel. I'm a sophomore at the University of Illinois at Urbana-Champaign, where I'm majoring in Biochemistry.

Last summer my brother and I went on a two-week, 180-mile sea kayaking trip on the west side of Prince William Sound. We flew to Anchorage, rented our kayaks, and then were driven to Portage, where caught a short train that goes through a long tunnel to Whittier. From Whittier we paddled out an 8-mile fiord that had fishing boat traffic, and after that, we didn't see much of anybody. Three days out we got to Harriman Fiord, which was like having Glacier Bay National Park to ourselves. The mountains go up to almost 10,000 feet, and glaciers pour off of them all the way to the water, where the ice breaks and falls with cannon roars. When I realized that the water was deep and the ice wouldn't produce tidal waves, I got up very close. The weather in Prince William Sound was better than I expected, and we had 3 sunny days--two in prime spots. We saw lots of wildlife--seals, sea otters, sea lions, bald eagles, bears, and a humpback whale.

FIGURE 2.2 Rachel Jones's home page

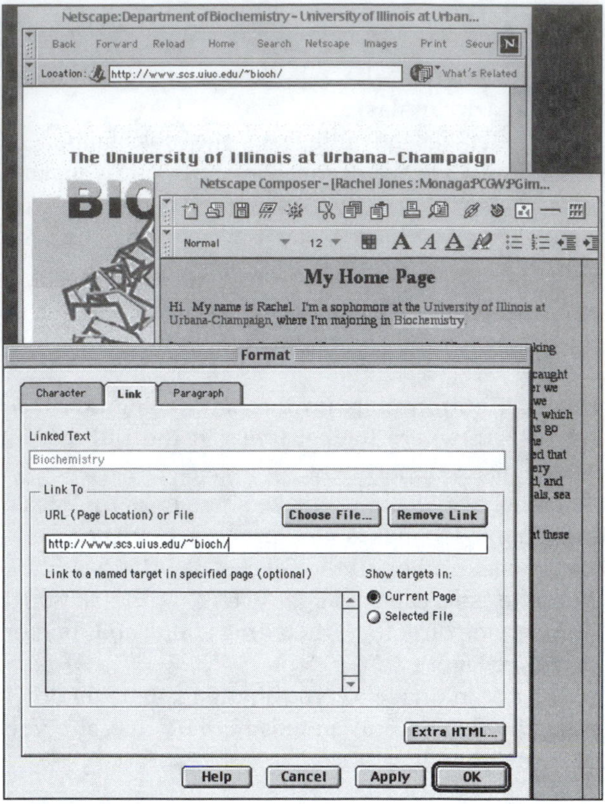

FIGURE 2.3 Link Dialog Box in Composer

Adding pictures

Rachel decides she wants a picture of a humpback whale. She remembers that the search engine Lycos has a gallery of images that can be legally copied (for more on the copyright issues involved in publishing images on the Web, see chapter 9). She switches to the Navigator window and searches for "humpback whale" on the Lycos site at http://www.lycos.com. Up pop two thumbnail images of humpback whales from the Alaska Division of Tourism. She views the image that she likes by clicking on it (see Figure 2.5). To copy the image to her page, she follows these steps:

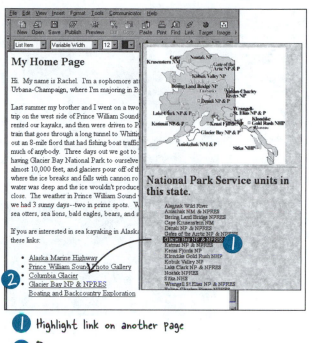

(1) Highlight link on another page

(2) Drag and drop on page

FIGURE 2.4   Dragging and dropping a link in Composer

1. Click the right mouse button (Windows) or hold down the mouse button (Macintosh) until a pop-up window appears.
2. Select **Copy this Image.**
3. Paste in the image just like text.

She also remembers to include the caption giving credit for the picture. She wants to distinguish the caption from her text, so she selects **Font** under the **Format** menu and picks Helvetica. She reduces the size from 12 to 9.

Customizing a page

With the basic elements of her page now assembled, Rachel can concentrate on improving the look of her page. She changes the gray background to white by following these steps:

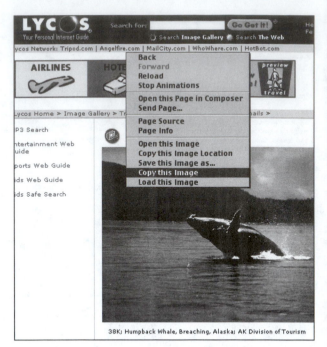

FIGURE 2.5   Copying an image in Navigator

1. Select **Page Properties** from the **Format** menu, which shows another dialog box.
2. Select **Use Custom Colors.**
3. Select a color (Rachel chooses **Black on Off-White** from the list).

Next, she makes the links into a bullet list. She highlights the list and then clicks on the **bullet list** icon on the Formatting Toolbar (see Figure 2.6). Rachel wants to put her email address at the bottom of her page. She first clicks on the **horizontal line** icon, which puts a line at the bottom of her page. Then she includes her email address.

Giving your page a title

There is one last important step–giving your page a title. The **Page Title** is different from both the file name and the heading on the page. The page title shows up on the frame at the top of the page. Giving

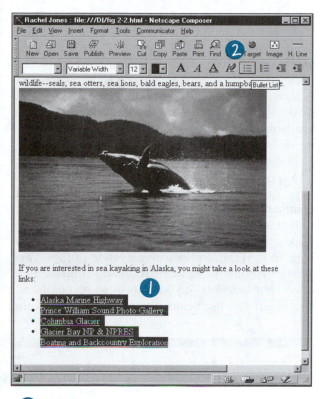

① Highlight list

② Click on the bullet list icon

FIGURE 2.6   Formatting a bullet list in Composer

your page an accurate title helps people when they bookmark a page to remember what's on it.

1. Select **Page Properties** from the **Format** menu.
2. Type the name of your page in the Title box.
3. Click OK.

Under the Hood: HTML Tags

In the 1920s, people who drove Model T Fords had to know how to fix them to keep them going. Today, with cars that go 100,000 miles without a tune-up, we don't spend much time under the hood. Nonetheless, it's good to know a little about how your car works, even if it's just to tell your mechanic what you think needs to be done. Similarly, fewer and fewer people now start by writing HTML when they compose a Web page, but knowing how HTML works enables you to make better use of the tools available on an editor and to troubleshoot if the editor doesn't produce exactly what you want.

In the early days of the Web, most people learned HTML by studying the HTML code on existing Web sites. Anyone can do this by using the **Page Source** command on the **View** menu (see Figure 2.7).

If you haven't looked at HTML before, it probably strikes you as complicated and messy, but there is a logic to it. HTML works with a system of tags. Tags generally come in pairs surrounding the text they affect. For example, if you want a word boldfaced, you insert the tag before the word to turn on the

```
Netscape
<HTML>
<HEAD>
    <META HTTP-EQUIV="Content-Type" CONTENT="text/html; charset=iso-8859-1">
    <META NAME="Author" CONTENT="UT Connect">
    <META NAME="GENERATOR" CONTENT="Mozilla/4.04 [en] (Win95; I) [Netscape]">
    <TITLE>Rachel Jones</TITLE>
</HEAD>
<BODY>

<H2>
My Home Page</H2>
Hi.  My name is Rachel.  I'm a sophomore at the University of
Illinois at Urbana-Champaign, where I'm majoring in Biochemistry.

<P>Last summer my brother and I went on a two-week, 180-mile sea kayaking
trip on the west side of Prince William Sound.  We flew to Anchorage,
rented our kayaks, and then were driven to Portage, where caught a short
train that goes through a long tunnel to Whittier.  From Whittier
we paddled out an 8-mile fiord that had fishing boat traffic, and after
that, we didn't see much of anybody.  Three days out we got to Harriman
Fiord, which was like having Glacier Bay National Park to ourselves. 
The mountains go up to almost 10,000 feet, and glaciers pour off of them
all the way to the water, where the ice breaks and falls with cannon roars.&nbs
When I realized that the water was deep and the ice wouldn't produce tidal
waves, I got up very close.  The weather in Prince William Sound was
better than I expected, and we had 3 sunny days--two in prime spots. 
We saw lots of wildlife--seals, sea otters, sea lions, bald eagles, bears,
and a humpback whale. <IMG SRC="whale.jpg" BORDER=0 HEIGHT=292 WIDTH=442>

<P>If you are interested in sea kayaking in Alaska, you might take a look
at these links:
<UL>
<LI>
<A HREF="http://www.dot.state.ak.us/external/amhs/general/geninfo.html">Alaska
Marine Highway</A></LI>

<LI>
<A HREF="http://www.gorp.com/gorp/location/ak/macgill/pwsgal.htm">Prince
William Sound Photo Gallery</A></LI>

<LI>
<A HREF="http://www.gorp.com/awss/pws.htm#anchor1140794">Columbia Glacier</A></
```

FIGURE 2.7 HTML source of Rachel's home page

boldfacing <B> and the tag after the word to turn off the boldfacing </B>. Most tags use this starting and closing formula to define areas of text. Your word processing program does something very similar but you never see the code. HTML editors like Netscape Composer allow you to see the code, and high-end editors like Macromedia Dreamweaver allow you to see both the page and the code at the same time.

Think of tags as the way the Web page file gives instructions to the browser. If Rachel were beginning her Web page from scratch, she would start by telling the browser that she is making an HTML document. Next she would put in a set of HEAD tags for the page title, which Rachel makes by inserting TITLE commands. Then she would be ready to start on the body—what actually shows up on the screen—so she adds the BODY tags.

```
<HTML>
<HEAD>
<TITLE>Rachel Jones</TITLE>
</HEAD>
<BODY>
[HTML for items actually appearing on the page]
</BODY>
</HTML>
```

Specifying colors

You can place **attributes** inside certain tags that affect how the tag is applied. For example, Rachel wants an off-white background instead of gray, so she changes the BODY tag to <BODY BGCOLOR= "FFF0F0">. FFF0F0 is the computer code for off-white. Netscape and Internet Explorer also allow you to use simple names such as "red" and "white." It's also possible to specify the color of links to change them from the default colors. The codes for the colors with color picker tools come with your editor or can be found many places on the Web. The link color commands also go in the BODY

tag and look like this <BODY BGCOLOR="FFF0F0"
LINK="#FF0000" VLINK="#800080"ALINK="#0000FF">.

```
<HTML>
<HEAD>
<TITLE>Rachel Jones</TITLE>
</HEAD>
<BODY BGCOLOR="FFFFFF" TEXT="#000000" LINK=
"#660000" VLINK="#0033CC" ALINK="#CCCCCC">
<H2> <CENTER> My Home Page </CENTER> </H2>
</BODY>
</HTML>
```

Formatting text

Rachel wants her heading at the top of the body and
she wants it centered. Notice how the center tags
are nested within the heading tags. You can keep
adding tags (<I> <U> <B> My Home Page </B>
</U> </I>), which would italicize, boldface, and
underline *__My Home Page,__* but it's important not to
overlap them. You don't want tags to look like this:
<I> <U> <B> My Home Page </I> </U> </B>. It
confuses the browser.

Now Rachel is ready to start typing in her text.
She types in the first two paragraphs.

```
<HTML>
<HEAD>
<TITLE>Rachel Jones</TITLE>
</HEAD>
<BODY BGCOLOR="FFFFFF" TEXT="#000000" LINK=
"#660000" VLINK="#0033CC" ALINK="#CCCCCC">
<H2> <CENTER> My Home Page </CENTER> </H2>
My name is Rachel. I'm a sophomore at the
University of Illinois at Urbana-Champaign, where
I'm majoring in Biochemistry.
Last summer my brother and I went on a two-
week, 180-mile sea kayaking trip on the west side
of Prince William Sound. [the text continues]
</BODY>
</HTML>
```

Viewing your page with a browser

To view your page, you must first save it. The name of the file must end in **.htm** or **.html**. (If you are using a word processing program for HTML coding, choose **save as** and select "text only"). Rachel saves her file as "index.html" and opens it in Navigator using the **Open Page** command. She doesn't like what she sees.

All of her text has flowed into one big paragraph because browsers don't recognize spacing and formatting. To tell the browser you're starting a paragraph, you have to use the <P> tag. The close paragraph </P> tag is optional. The <P> tag places an extra line between paragraphs, which makes prose quite readable on a computer screen. If you do not want a blank line inserted, use the line break tag <BR>.

"It's not a place
To go to twice," he says
And goes three times.

Fonts in HTML

Web page editors including Netscape Composer allow you to control the typeface, size, and color of the fonts your visitors will see. These changes are controlled by <FONT> commands. For example, if Rachel wanted the word Alaska to jump off the page, she might make it bigger, change the color to red, and change the font face to a contrasting font. For the contrasting font, she wants Arial. So the command would look like: <FONT SIZE="+1" COLOR= "#CC0000"FACE="ARIAL">Alaska</FONT>.

> ✓ When you make changes and want to view them with your browser, you have to save your file first and then click on the **Reload** button. Sometimes you have to hold down the Shift or Option key when you click Reload to get the new version.

Adding links

Adding links to your site often results in problems, so proceed with care. Let's start with the link to Rachel's major department, Biochemistry. Begin by surrounding the area you want to specify as the clickable link with the <A> tag: <A>Biochemistry </A>. Next add the URL (the address of the page you want to link to) using the HREF attribute within the opening <A> tag:

<A HREF="http://www.scs.uiuc.edu/~bioch/"> Biochemistry</A>.

Long URLs often lead to typos. You have to be 100% accurate when you type in a URL or else the browser won't find it. URLs are case sensitive on many servers, which means that if you name your file "Whale.html" and make the link to "whale.html," the browser will not find it. When you name files, use only lower case and you'll avoid the problem of capital letters causing broken links.

Absolute vs. relative links

There are two kinds of links: links to other pages on your Web site and links to other sites on the Web. When you link to other locations, such as the biochemistry department site, you must give the full

URL. These links are called **absolute links.** But when you link to other pages on your site, you can and should use a partial URL. If the link is in the same folder as your HTML file, you need only use the file name. These links are called **relative links.** For example, if Rachel posted another page about the whale she saw, the link would look like this: <A HREF="whale.html">humpback whale</A>. When you're building a small site, using fewer than thirty files, keep all your files in the same folder and use relative links. Relative links allow your site to load faster and make it easier for you when you put your site on the server.

Adding images

Web browsers can read images in two formats: GIF and JPEG (see chapter 3 for more on preparing images). You can tell if your image is in one of these formats by looking at the end of the file name; files ending with .gif or .jpg should display on a browser. Tell the browser to include images on your page with an <IMG> tag. Rachel saves the image of the humpback whale to her hard drive in the same folder as her HTML file. She adds it to her page with this tag: <IMG SRC="whale.jpg">. The picture is jammed up next to the text. The problem can be fixed by adding a paragraph command between the text and the picture <P>. Now the spacing looks right, but the image is still too big for her page (see Figure 2.8).

You can specify the width and height of an image in **pixels.** (A **pixel** is a dot on a picture that is the basic unit of images.) Putting in height and width dimensions also makes the page load faster because the browser doesn't have to compute the size of the image. The image is 442 × 292 pixels, so Rachel decides to center the image and reduce the size to roughly a third by specifying the dimensions <CENTER> <IMG SRC="whale.jpg" WIDTH=295 HEIGHT=195></CENTER> (see Figure 2.9).

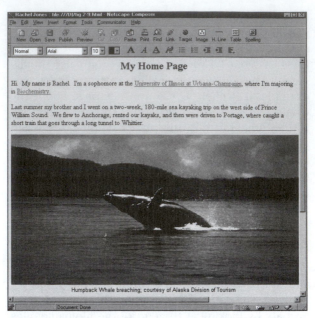

FIGURE 2.8 Image of whale without width and height specified

When you might hand code HTML instead of using an editor

You may be asking at this point why you should go to this much trouble writing HTML when the editor does it for you. Resizing images is one example of why it is handy to know a little about how HTML works. You can do some resizing with an editor that gives you handles on the edges of images, but specifying the size commands in pixels puts you in complete control.

Netscape and Internet Explorer allow you to size images in pixels and to build space around your images. Sometimes an image is slightly too big for where it is supposed to fit, and being able to trim a few pixels gets it exactly right. Sometimes images appear jammed up against text. The HSPACE and VSPACE attributes leave some blank space around the image. For example, if you want to have five pix-

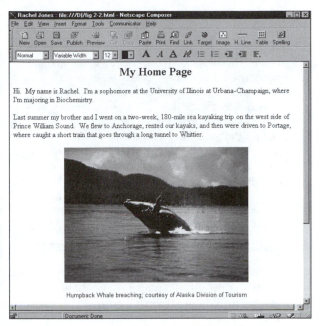

FIGURE 2.9   Image of whale with width and height specified

els of blank space around the top, bottom, and sides of an image, you can insert these attributes <IMG SRC="whale.jpg" HSPACE=5 VSPACE=5>. Knowing HTML allows you to tweak your page.

Another reason it's handy to know some HTML is that editors don't always do everything you want them to do. For example, you might want to include a link that sends mail to your email address. Most Web page editors can do this for you, but Composer does not have this feature. So Rachel might include a tag to make it easy to send her mail: Send mail to <A HREF="mailto:rachel.jones@uiuc.edu">Rachel </A>. Composer allows you to insert HTML tags with the command **HTML Tag** on the **Insert** menu.

Still another reason is that editors try to do things for you that you don't necessarily want. Sometimes the spacing seems way off, and often the problem is that the editor has forced in some extra

---

THE W3C CONSORTIUM

No one is in charge of the Web, but a group of representatives from universities, Web designers, and software companies form the World Wide Web Consortium or W3C. This group issued the first standards for HTML in 1995 and has been revising the guidelines ever since. In 1998, W3C released the guidelines for HTML 4.0, which includes the specifications for style sheets (see chapter 4). The W3C Web site (http://www. w3.org) has many valuable resources, including a complete list of HTML commands and guidelines for designing Web sites for users with disabilities.

---

spaces with the command ** .** When you think some extra, unwanted spaces have been added, open the file and delete them. Of course you can add them too.

There are many more HTML commands, but once you know how they work, you can figure out ones you haven't seen before. (See Appendix B for a list.) We're getting close to never needing to look at HTML in composing for the Web, but we're not quite there yet.

Putting Your Pages on Your Server

When you've set up an account on a server and you have a Web page ready to go, the next step is getting it on the Web. Web page editors make this process easy after you have your account set up on a Web server. On Netscape Composer click on the Publish icon. Make sure you've given your page a title and a name ending in **.htm** or **.html** extension so that a browser can recognize it as a Web page.

Next enter the location of where you're going to publish your Web page. If you are using a server at your college or university, you were given this address when you set up your account. Rachel's server address is http://students.uiuc.edu. If you are using an Internet service provider like AOL, your server address might begin something like ftp://ftp.aol.com/docs/. Netscape Composer and other Web page editors remember this address, so if you are using only one server, you don't have to type it again. In Composer click on **Use Default Location** on the dialog box the next time you want to send a file to the server.

Next type in your user name and password. If your pages are on your own computer, click on **Save Password** so you don't have to retype your password every time. Composer will also send along files associated with your page, including image files. When Rachel sends her index.html to the server, Composer takes whale.jpg with it so the picture of the whale can appear on her page (see Figure 2.10). When you make changes on a file and send it again to the server, the revised file will replace the old file. Unlike your home computer, though, you won't get a warning that the old file is being discarded.

The alternative way of getting files on a server is to use a **file transfer protocol** or **ftp** program. Before Web page editors came along, ftp programs were the only way you could put files on a server from a remote location. The most popular ftp program on Windows is WS_FTP and on Macintosh is Fetch. Both are easy after you practice a time or two, but it helps to have someone walk you through them the first time.

Organizing Your Web Site

Web sites often take on a life of their own when you start one. For many people, building an extensive Web site becomes a personal hobby. Others become involved in building a large Web site to support an organization they belong to or even as an

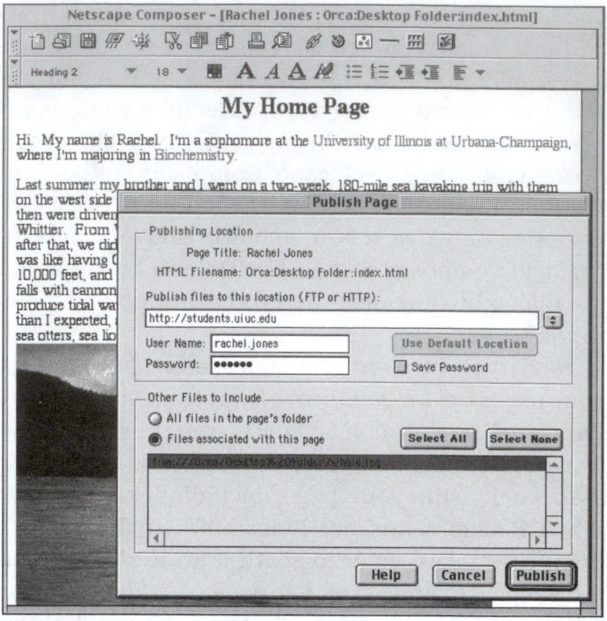

FIGURE 2.10 Publish Page dialog box on Composer

opportunity to run a small business. When you start building a site with several pages, the files multiply in a hurry. Remember, each image is a separate file. In addition to pictures, you might want to make icons for making links instead of words. Each one of those icons is a separate file. Imagine what your personal computer at home would be like if you didn't have folders to manage all that you accumulated. It would be tough to sort through all your files each time you wanted to find something. The same is true of your files on a server. Once you start putting many files on a server, sorting them out becomes a problem.

You can organize files in folders on the server just as you can on your home computer. Files are much easier to keep track of this way. Furthermore, you can upload an entire site, so what's on the server is organized the same way it is on your home machine. Typically people start off by putting every-thing in the same folder. Rachel's index.html has one image file associated, and if both were on the desktop of her home computer and she sent them both to the server, they would look like this:

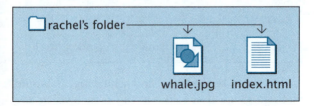

If Rachel were handcoding her file, the link to the image file on index.html would be <IMG SRC="whale.jpg">.

   It's fine to put everything in the same folder for a small site. But when a site starts growing and you start adding a lot of images, it quickly becomes messy. A good way to begin to manage the prolifer-ation of files is to put all the image files into a folder named "images." Rachel could make an images fold-er and put whale.jpg in it:

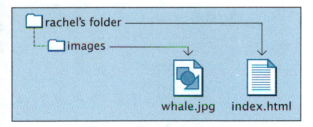

Using an images folder, however, requires telling the browser that whale.jpg is in a different folder. The command <IMG SRC="images/whale.jpg"> means that whale.jpg is in a folder named "images."

   Let's say that Rachel plans to put other Web sites on her account and wants to keep the files that cre-ate her home page in a folder called "home." She wants to keep her images in a separate folder. So her directory would look like this:

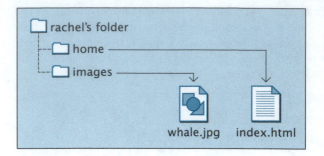

In order for a browser to find whale.jpg, it would have to go to another folder at the same level as the "home" folder that contains index.html. The command <IMG SRC="../images/whale.jpg"> means go up one level, then find the folder images and then the file whale.jpg. If an image doesn't show up when you put the site on the server, it's probably because you haven't given the browser the correct instructions to find it. These problems are usually easy to fix if you have a basic knowledge of how HTML works.

Stay Organized

- **Figure out your system for naming files.** Use only lower case letters because you will eventually get confused if you use capitals. Don't put any spaces or characters like semicolons file names because they cause problems for servers. All Web pages must end in **.htm** or **.html**. Label image files by their type, either **.gif** (for GIF files) or **.jpg** (for JPEG files).

- **Put your files in a folder.** Put the files on your Web site server in a folder just like you do on your computer. The simplest way is to move the entire folder to the server when you are ready.

- **Use relative links.** Use relative links giving only the file name for files on your site (or folder and file names if you put some files in a separate folder), so all your links will work when you put it on the server or move it to a different server. If you make absolute links that give the full name of the server for the files on your site, the links will not work if you change servers.

- **Save, Save, Save.** It is always a good idea to make back-up copies. You should make copies on a diskette or even better, on a zip disk.

Steps in Creating a Web Site

The Design Side

A Web Site as Architecture

Web sites are described with metaphors of place. You *visit* a *home* page, *navigate* on a Web *site*, participate in a *community*, *travel* on the *information highway*, and *explore worlds*. These metaphors are not accidental. The visual interface that we take for granted today marked a great breakthrough in computing because it allowed knowledge to be categorized and accessed in visual as well as verbal forms. At first, this visual potential was largely limited to the familiar desktop icons of folders and trash cans. With the Web we see some of this visual potential realized with representations of living rooms, houses, town squares, Middle Eastern bazaars, museums, parks, and a great deal more. It's no wonder that people associate the Web with places because you do move through a geography of images, information, sound,

CHAPTER 3

and video. If the current generation of video games are an indication of where the Web is headed, these virtual places will seem far more real and immediate in the near future.

As writers we have been taught to think of beginnings, middles, and endings. Places, however, often do not have clear beginnings, middles, and especially endings. Instead we enter a Web site much as we enter a building, and when we're inside, we make a decision about how to move through the building or else we turn around and leave. Because people experience the Web as spatial, we have a great deal to learn from those who design spaces for people. Buildings that have been in use for many decades and even centuries survive not only because they are structurally sound. Successful buildings endure because they are functional; they provide spaces well suited for the activities that take place there. The best buildings are also aesthetically pleasing. We might then define architecture as functional art. Builders of Web sites also combine art and technology to create functional art. They are, like architects, creators of spaces that people interact with and move through—spaces that can be both practical and beautiful.

Successful architects begin by envisioning how people will use a building and how they will encounter and move through it. Architects have long understood the critical importance of entrances and use them to convey much more than going simply from outside to inside. The triumphal arches of ancient Rome were designed to impress all those who passed under them of the greatness of the Roman Empire. Often the effects of entrances, however, are created with subtlety. The anonymous architect who designed the Mission Espiritu Santo in East Texas in the mid-1700s did not want parishioners to approach the entrance directly (see Figure 3.1). Instead they would have to contemplate the grandeur of the building before turning gradually to the entrance. Then a few more steps are required until the intimate carvings surrounding the doorway come into focus. Even

FIGURE 3.1   Approach and doorway of Mission Espiritu Santo (1749) near Goliad, Texas (Photos by author)

today the entrance to the mission evokes a sense of entering a sacred, mystical space.

No part of a Web site is more important than the entrance. This first page is a portal that users pass through to get inside the site. What users expect to find on a site and how they expect to interact with the site are shaped by the initial page. Designers of Web sites sometimes draw directly on the work of architects in constructing entryways for Web sites. The entry page for the Metropolitan Museum of Art in New York City represents the entrance to the building and offers thumbnails of the great art inside (see Figure 3.2).

After an architect imagines a visitor entering a building, she must next decide how to lead that visitor through the building. The Metropolitan Museum of Art has a complicated floor plan; for those unfamiliar with the museum a map is required to locate a specific piece of art (see Figure 3.3). Because the Metropolitan Museum is one of the largest art museums in the world, it's not surprising that navigating through it would be relatively complex. You might have to walk through several rooms and make sev-

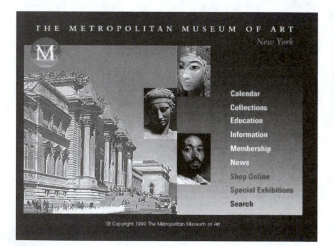

FIGURE 3.2 Metropolitan Museum of Art, New York (http://www.metmuseum.org/)

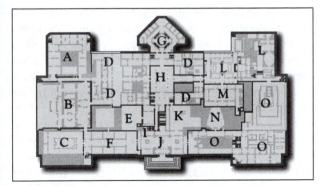

FIGURE 3.3 Plan of the First Floor, Metropolitan Museum of Art, New York

eral turns before you find a single piece of art you want to see.

Some Web sites also require you to make several moves before you reach a particular page. As a site designer, you may offer few choices on any one page and require your visitors to click through several pages before reaching a specific page. We might describe such a structure as narrow and deep (see Figure 3.4).

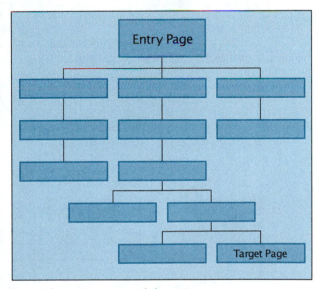

FIGURE 3.4 A narrow and deep site structure

In contrast to the museum architecture, a shopping mall typically arranges stores along corridors so that they are easy to access. A corresponding Web site structure would present many choices on the entry page and give access to all pages with a click or two. We might describe this structure as broad and shallow (see Figure 3.5).

For another type of Web site structure, imagine that you are at a party with a lot of people you know. You talk to many different people, but the order is not predictable. You see an old friend on the other side of the room, and you know you will find her eventually, but it takes a while before you get over there and you end up meeting some new people on the way. Hypertext structures often work in similar ways (see Figure 3.6). A hypertext structure is still ordered—you eventually get to a certain Web page—but it can allow many different paths to reach the same place.

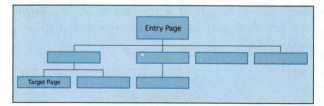

FIGURE 3.5 A broad and shallow site structure

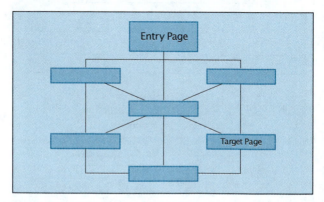

FIGURE 3.6 A hypertext structure

The kind of structure you design determines how visitors will experience your Web site. It should reflect the experience you want to create.

Establish Your Goals

Good architects begin by asking who will use a building and what will they use it for. Good writers ask similar questions: Who is likely to read what I write? and What am I trying to accomplish? Even if you are writing a diary only for yourself, you still ask these questions in some way. If, for example, you are writing a journal during a trip you take, you might record where exactly you went, how long it took to get there, and how much you spent. Or you might concentrate on describing in detail what you saw and who you met. Or you might focus on your reactions to particular places and people. You run into similar issues when you put up a Web site.

First, what do you want your Web site to do?

In the early days of the Web, the main purpose was **informative**—to make scientific papers quickly and easily available to other researchers. After browsers made the Web easy to use, companies rushed to the Web to advertise and later for e-commerce. Many organizations advocating particular causes also put up sites. Even though these sites display a wide range of goals, their general purpose is **persuasive;** they want you to buy something or believe something. Individuals also put up many thousands of Web pages early on and haven't slowed down—some informative, some persuasive, but many for the fun of it—to display art work, to post a family album, to list personal interests in the hope of meeting like-minded people, to tell a little about themselves. We might classify these sites as **self expressive.**

What's your main goal? What personality do you want your site to project? What "look" and "feel" do you want your site to possess?

Second, who do you want to visit your site?

Many times when you write on paper, you have a good sense of who will read it. For example, if you write an editorial for your college newspaper, you expect other students, faculty, administrators, and people interested in your school to be your readers. And when you write a paper for a course, you know the only reader likely will be your instructor. But when you put up a Web site, even one that fulfills a course requirement, you cannot be quite so sure who will visit it. Many students have had the experience of receiving email from people in other countries only hours after putting up a site in a trial version. Search engines turn up sites according to key words, so if you have a name or phrase on your site that someone is looking for, the search engine will find it. Perhaps you don't care about these visitors, but that's what makes the Web different from any previous publishing medium: millions of people from around the world have the potential to view your site. Many people who put up Web sites go to great effort to attract many visitors and put counters on their sites to keep track of hits.

Are you aiming your site at a target group of viewers? Would you like to have a lot of different people visit your site? Will visitors need high-speed connections to the Internet to see all that's on your site? Do you want people with relatively slow telephone modem connections to be able to access your site?

Third, what do you want visitors to do when they get to your site?

Do you want them simply to read the text you have put up? Do you want them to navigate around on your site? Do you want them to follow the links to other Web sites that you have made? If they click on the links to other Web sites, do you want them to come back to your site? Do you want them to write anything, such as make an entry in a guest book? Do you want them to send you email? However you answer these questions, you should make it obvious to visitors how they might use your site.

Defining specific goals

How you answer these questions is crucial in determining how you envision your Web site. Often it is hard to articulate a vision of what you want to achieve in precise terms. To begin to translate a vision into specific goals, it is useful to think about your own experiences on the Web. You might start out by making two lists: 1) What you hate about your least favorite sites, and 2) What you like about your favorite sites. Your "hate" list might look something like this:

Web sites I hate

1. Too slow. Sites take too long to appear.

2. Can't find what I'm looking for on a site.

3. Pages are too crowded, hard to read.

4. Too many bells and whistles like Java applets and animations that take forever to download and don't add anything.

5. Hard to navigate within a site.

6. Poorly written content with many errors.

Some of these items might sound like technical issues, but in fact they are all design issues. If you put huge image files on your Web pages, the time it takes for a telephone modem user to download your site will be excruciating. In many cases unnecessary graphics and complicated backgrounds contribute to the crowding. Even when a site is visually appealing, if the organization of the site is jumbled and the text poorly written, the site seems sloppy and poorly executed.

By contrast your list of what you like about your favorite Web sites might look like this:

Web sites I like

1. If necessary I can turn off the images on a site and still use it, allowing it to load fast.

2. Information I want is easy to find.

3. Content is up-to-date and interesting.

4. Site is visually attractive.

5. Navigation is easy—always a way back to the start and to other major parts of the site.

6. Text is well written.

On a well designed site, the images contribute to the overall effect without calling unnecessary attention to themselves. Information on the site be located without difficulty so if you return to the site later, you don't have the frustrating experience of being unable to find something you have seen before. The best Web sites reflect a great deal of attention to detail. You should include in your goals the characteristics of Web sites that you find most appealing. You want your Web site to be handsome, well organized, easy to navigate, informative, and well written.

Develop Your Workplan

You may be building a Web site as part of a team or doing it yourself, but in either case, you need to start out with a plan.

1. Articulate your goals

After you've had a chance to think through what you want your Web site to do and you have a vision of your site in mind, then it's time to list the goals that will achieve that vision. The more specific you can make these goals, the more helpful they will be.

2. Categorize your target audience

How familiar will the members of your target audience be with the subject of your site? How much background do you need to provide? What is their age range? What is their level of computer experience and experience surfing the Web? Will most have fast or slow connections to the Web? What can you anticipate about their content expectations? What can you anticipate about their technical expectations?

3. Determine what content you need and how you will obtain it

What content needs to go on your site? Where will you find the content? How much can you rely on personal experience? How much of the information you need can be found on the Web? In libraries? By talking to people? By conducting experimental or survey research? If you are working as a team, you need to determine who will be responsible for what areas.

4. Determine the structure of your site

It's a good idea to make a map of your site as you develop the content. Often it is best to plan this structure on a big sheet of paper with large sticky notes which you can move around. Your map should show all the pages on your site and which pages will be linked.

5. Determine what kinds of navigational tools you will need

You have several decisions to make, which will be discussed in more detail in Chapter 5. You have to decide how to allow visitors to move through your site and what tools to provide them. Navigation tools can take the form of menu bars, buttons, clickable images, or links in text.

6. Determine a visual theme for your site based on the content

Having a consistent look to your pages is not only attractive. It gives your site continuity and lets visitors know that they are still on your site, especially if you have links that go to other Web sites. Determine the visual theme for your site early on and make a template for your content pages. That way you don't have to type in the same information over and over about background and font colors, navigation tools, and other identical features.

7. Determine the file structure for your site and give the files meaningful names

Remember that the file structure of your site is not going to correspond exactly to the page structure. Any images that you have on your Web pages will be separate files, and you may want to put all image files in a separate folder. (See "Organizing Your Web Site," pp. 39–43.) Name your files in such a way that you can remember what they are. If you have several images and you name them **image01.jpg**, **image02.jpg**, and so on, soon you will have to open the file to remember what's on it. If you give files names that indicate the content (**dolphin.jpg**), they are much easier to keep track of when you are making links.

8. Think about how the site might change over time and plan for change

Web sites often grow over time. Beginning with a long-term plan allows you to add to the site and revise it. Redoing all the menus on a large site each time you add a new page can quickly become an ordeal. If you think ahead about where any new pages might go, you often can anticipate what changes you will need to make in menus and navigation tools.

9. Allow time for testing and improving the site

Good Web sites cannot be done at the last minute. You will need to plan enough time to do a thorough review of your site yourself and gather feedback from others.

Compose for Online Environments

When you write for the world of print, you expect that if your readers are interested, they will read all that you write from beginning to end. Actual readers often do not read from front to back in a straight line, but the technology of print is designed for reading an entire book or an article in a newspaper or magazine continuously. While it's possible to go back and forth in print, the basic movement in print is linear and the basic unit is the paragraph. By contrast, the basic movement on the Web is nonlinear and the basic unit is the screen. Perhaps the most important fact to remember is many users don't scroll down the first page. Their eyes stop at the bottom of the screen. And those who do scroll down usually don't scroll down very long; three screens is about the maximum. If you have a lot of text that you want to put on a Web site, you have to plan your strategy carefully.

The first screen is the most important

People who browse Web sites don't hang around long if they aren't interested or if it takes too long to find out what's on the Web site. That's why the first screen is critical. If you have something important to tell your visitors, tell them right away. They probably aren't going to click through a bunch of screens or scroll though long stretches to find out what your site is about. Furthermore, they are not likely to wait indefinitely for your site to load if you put big image files on your first page. Text loads much faster than images, which is why the words you put on your first page are so important. Visitors can read the text on a page while the images are loading.

The text on your first page should convey what can be found on your site and who might be interested in it. For example, the first page of the Department of Advertising's Web site tells where it is located geographically and within the University of Texas, that the department offers courses for both graduate and undergraduate students, and that the site contains information about the advertising industry and research in advertising in addition to information about the department (see Figure 3.7).

The navigation tools running down the left side of the first page are keyed off this text. If a visitor is more interested in the advertising industry than the Department of Advertising, she will know to click on "Advertising World."

Divide your text into chunks if possible

Long stretches of text on the Web tend not to get read. Without a large-screen monitor, reading text on the Web is like trying to read a newspaper through a 3" square hole. It's possible to do but not much fun. Newspapers grew to their present size because our eyes can take in a large expanse of information when we scan the page. Perhaps in the next few years, large-screen monitors will give us an expanse of screen real estate comparable to a news-paper page, but in the meantime, most Web users will still have small-screen monitors, often made even smaller when people do not resize their browsers to fit the entire screen or leave visible all the toolbars. You have to design your page for the small screen.

Whenever possible, many Web designers try to divide text into chunks that fit on a screen or require

FIGURE 3.7   First page for the Department of Advertising, University of Texas at Austin (http://advertising.utexas.edu)

minimal scrolling down. For example, a site on The Biology Place designed by Graham Kent explains the process of cellular respiration where the chemical energy in glucose is released and partially converted into ATP. This site uses both text and images to present a key concept on a succession of screens (see Figure 3.8).

There are advantages and disadvantages associated with putting text on the Web. An advantage is the ability to put a great deal of background information on a Web site connected by links to the main text. You can design a single site for those who know a great deal about the subject and can skip the background information, and for those who know little and need the background. The big disadvantage is that it's more difficult to place a long text on the Web in a form that people will read. Some Web designers don't even try. They assume that those who are really interested will download that long text, print it, and read it on paper. That assumption, however, risks losing people who don't want to take the time to print a long text. There are some ways to make a long text more readable on a screen. It helps to narrow the line width. You'll find out how to divide a text into columns in Chapter 4. Shorter

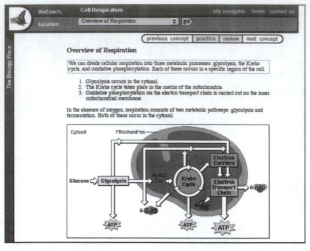

FIGURE 3.8   Cell Respiration: Overview of Respiration

paragraphs with more white space also aid readability. Paragraphs should run a maximum of eight lines. If they run longer, break them into more manageable units. Another key factor is to select a readable font, which we'll turn to now.

Select fonts wisely and make your text readable

Until computers and word processing software came along, most writers had little or no control over type styles, which are called **fonts.** If they typed, they probably used Courier without knowing that it had a special name. But if writers knew little about fonts and other aspects of printing before computers came along, printers had five hundred years of experience learning about which fonts are easiest to read and what effects different fonts produce. Fonts are described according to families, and the two most important families are **serif** and **sans serif** fonts. Serif (rhymes with "sheriff") fonts were developed first, imitating the strokes of an ink pen. Serifs are the little wedge-shaped ends on letter forms, which scribes produced with wedge-tipped pens. Serif fonts also have thick and thin transitions on the curved strokes, again imitating the pen. Three of the most common serif fonts are:

Times
Palatino
Bookman

If these fonts look almost alike to you, it's not an accident. Serif fonts were designed to be easy to read in printed text.

Sans serif fonts ("sans" is French for "without") don't have the little wedge-shape ends on letters and the thickness of the letters is the same. Popular sans serif fonts include:

Helvetica
Avant Garde
Arial

Sans serif fonts work well for headings and short stretches of text, giving a crisp, modern look. Sans serif fonts are easier to read than serif fonts on a Web page. Sans serif fonts require fewer pixels and thus have better resolution than serif fonts. Thus sans serif fonts look sharper on the screen.

Above all, your text should be readable. Remember that dark backgrounds make for tough reading. If you use a dark background and want people to read what you write, be sure to increase the font size, make sure the contrast between font and background is adequate, and avoid using all caps and italics.

> **TEXT IN ALL CAPS IS HARD TO READ ON A BLACK BACKGROUND, *ESPECIALLY IF THE TEXT IS IN ITALICS.***

Choose your background and text colors carefully if you want to increase readability. Bizarre combinations like blue on magenta can have an impact, but they are not pleasant to read for long. Likewise, using the wrong background graphics can be distracting and can make your text hard to read. If you use a background graphic, make sure it stays in the background.

Anticipate users' questions

Many Web sites include a Questions and Answers page or a FAQ (Frequently Asked Questions) to address questions users may ask. This strategy also can be used to present content that lends itself well to a question and answer structure. Mike Atkinson uses this structure for discussing current issues in psychology (see Figure 3.9).

The Question and Answer structure allows users to select what they want to know most about. It also helps in dividing text into blocks that fit on a single screen.

Test and improve your site

Good Web sites take time to complete. Nothing is more aggravating on the Web (aside from not being able to get on) than a Web site with broken links, numerous errors, and entire sections "under construction." Before you upload your site to the server, you should make sure all your links are working and everything appears the way you want it to appear. If possible, you should load your folder on a different platform (e.g., on Windows if you composed it on a Mac), you should look at your site on different screen sizes (e.g., 640×480, 832×624), and you should try it with both Netscape and Internet Explorer. Remember, different people will visit your site on different computers using different browsers with different connections to the Internet, and all these variables will affect how your site will be viewed.

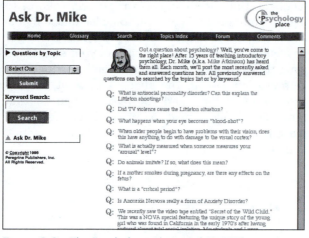

FIGURE 3.9 The Psychology Place: Ask Dr. Mike

Next you are ready to make a thorough review of your content. What kind of experience do you want to create and for whom? Does your site convey that experience to the people you want to visit your site? If your site is largely informative, how much do you need to explain the subject of your Web site? If you cite other work, is it clear where that work came from and can a user find it?

Now look at the appearance of your site. What visual message does it convey? Is the text easy to read? If you use a background, does it add to the site? How can you improve the appearance of your site? Consider, too, the navigation. Do you always know where you are in the site? Can you always get back to the start? Is it easy to move from one page to the other?

When you have done a thorough "in-house" review and made the necessary changes, it's time to put the site on your server. By putting the site on your server, you've declared that it's ready for the world to see. You should have on your site your email address or a way of getting in touch with you. A few people at least will give you some unsolicited feedback. But you should also ask specific people to look at your site and give you some feedback. If possible, ask people who are not in your class but might have some interest in the subject of your site. Often what they have to say will be extremely valuable in getting your site in the shape you want it. This process takes time, and you have to plan for that time. The biggest mistake professional designers make is not allowing time for the process of testing and improving.

ASK USERS FOR FEEDBACK ON YOUR WEB SITE

1. **Audience:** How does the site identify its intended audience? How well does it indicate what is on the site? NOTE: *Are there any ways that the site could be changed to maintain the user's interest?*

2. **Content:** How informative is the content? Where might more content be added? What do you want to know more about? Are there any mechanical, grammar, or style problems? NOTE: *What would most improve the content?*

3. **Readability:** Is there sufficient contrast between the text and the background to make it legible? Are the margins wide enough? Are there any paragraphs that go on too long and need to be divided? Are headings inserted in the right places, and if headings are used for more than one level, are these levels indicated consistently? Is high contrast text, including boldfacing and all caps, kept short? NOTE: *What might be done to make the text easier to read?*

4. **Visual Design:** Does the site have a consistent visual theme? Where is the focal point on each page? Do the images contribute to the visual appeal or do they detract from it? NOTE: *What would give the site more visual interest?*

5. **Navigation:** How easy or difficult is it to move from one page to another on the site? Is a consistent navigation scheme used throughout the site? Are there any broken links? NOTE: *Can the navigation be made easier?*

Visual Design for the Web

Principles of Visual Design

If a good Web site integrates technology, art, and writing, then good design is what makes it possible. You experience design almost every minute you are awake. On your campus or in the city or town where you live, there are some buildings that you always enjoy walking into and others that make you feel lost or seem sterile and ugly. These responses are a direct result of the design of a building. Unfortunately, design is rarely taught outside of specialized disciplines and is an uncomfortable word for most people who have not had formal training in art or a discipline that teaches design.

Language and visual design work in fundamentally different ways. Language is well adapted for talking about things that fall into a linear order. Because we perceive time as linear, language allows us from a very young age to tell stories. If you are describing a place, you have to decide what to tell about first. Suppose a friend asks you to describe a park in your city that she wants to visit by car. You might begin by telling her where to park and where to walk to, starting with the large swimming pool. But if you have a map to give to your friend, she can see at once how the park is laid out. That's the basic difference between describing with spoken language and describing with visual images. Spoken language forces you to put things in a *sequence*; visual design forces you to place things in *space*. As is the case for language, a few principles underlie visual design. Being aware of these principles will make you a more effective Web designer.

Know your visual message

What immediate reaction do you want to create when your page first appears on a user's screen? How will you convey visually what your site is about? If your site involves organizations, activities or products that can be represented well by images, such as a whitewater club Web site below, then this question is easily answered.

But suppose you are building a site for a project on business ethics. Would you use an image on the first page? What fonts and background color would you select? You can make your site look formal or informal, businesslike or casual, active or static, friendly or distant, bright or subdued. What personality do you want your site to have?

Create a visual theme for your site

A consistent look and feel makes your Web site appear unified and supports your content. You don't have to have a loud background or a lot of flash to achieve a visual theme. In fact, it's the little things—like selecting a simple set of colors for your text, headings, links, and background—that do more to create a consistent visual theme than does an attention-getting graphic. Consistency in navigation tools, discussed in the next chapter, is one of the most important aspects of the visual theme. The navigation bar should be placed at the top or on the side of the page, not at the bottom of a long page where a user must scroll down to find it. Similar graphics and images should be the same size, and often their placement can be repeated from page to page.

Another simple but important tactic is to identify each page either with a logo or a common header. The pages on the extensive Division of Rhetoric and Composition site use a common header with the name of the unit on top and a triangle in the upper right corner (see Figure 4.1). There's also contact information at the bottom of the each page along with consistent menu design on the left side.

Direct the eyes of the user

You should think about where you want the focal point of your pages to be, what you want to surround that focal point, and how you want to frame the page. Any motion on a page will get the user's attention first, so if you put animations on your page, they shouldn't be there just for ornament. Lacking motion on a page, images will draw attention next. If a page contains mostly text and does not

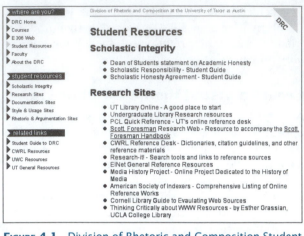

FIGURE 4.1   Division of Rhetoric and Composition Student Resources Page (http://www.drc.utexas.edu/stures/)

have a visual center, then readers of English and other European languages begin at the top left of the page. Remember that many users skim text on the Web so what gets read on your page depends a great deal on how you direct the user's eyes.

Avoid clutter

The limited screen real estate on the Web is a major headache for novice and professional designers alike. The temptation is to get everything on one page, but this strategy quickly leads to disaster. The Time-Warner Pathfinder site in 1997 had links on the main page to the many Time-Warner publications along with top news stories. The result was overwhelming (see Figure 4.2).

Clutter creeps into less extensive Web sites through decorative images that do not contribute to the content, distracting backgrounds, sprawling text that runs across the screen, and annoying animations and blinking texts. Blank space is an important design element. If you fill up a page, you risk elements competing against each other so intensely that the overall effect is chaotic.

FIGURE 4.2   Time-Warner Pathfinder site, May 15, 1997 (no longer available)

Achieve balance

Balance does not mean symmetry. Many beginning Web authors try to center everything, which leads to a dull, predictable design. Try making a sketch of your page first, using the equivalent of a 640×480 screen. Draw lines that divide your page into equal thirds horizontally and vertically. Place your key elements along these lines rather than in the center. This simple scheme can often produce striking results.

Communicate with Images and Graphics

Web page editors make it easy for you to put pictures and graphics on your Web site. You can find pictures and graphics in clip rrt files and on the Web, but you should always check the permission status when downloading an image, and you should be sure to give credit to the creator of an image. You can create your own digital images by using a photo processor that offers digital service. It's also easy to scan your own photographs. Computer labs often have scanners, and because scanners have become affordable, many people now own them. Maybe you have one too.

Using a scanner

If you are new to scanning, the complicated part is knowing what settings to use. Most of the time you can use the default settings and get reasonably good results (see Figure 4.3). One setting to pay close attention to is **dpi** (dots per inch). Remember that the Web can display only 72 dpi, so eventually you will need to reduce the resolution to 72 dpi. If you want to print the image, a higher resolution will produce a sharper image, but also a much bigger file. Here's how to scan an image for use on a Web page:

1. Place the photograph or drawing on the scanner bed and close the cover.
2. Select **Acquire** from the **File** menu and drag right to select the capture option for your scanner (for example, "UMAX magic scan").
3. Configure the settings in the dialog box.
   • Select either **Color, Gray** (for black and white images), or **Lineart** (for drawings).
   • Set the media for Reflective if you are scanning a photograph.
   • Set the resolution to 150 dpi (you can reduce it later) and the scaling to 100%.
   • Select **Preview** to view what you have placed on the scanner.
4. Use the rectangle tool to select the area you want to capture.
5. Select **Scan.** It may take a few minutes to scan the image. When scanning is finished, the image will appear in your photo editing program (e.g., Adobe Photoshop).
6. Select **Save As** and choose one of the two image formats that work best with all Web browsers: **GIF** and **JPEG.**

GIF images

Most images on the Web are in Graphics Interchange Format (GIF), which squeezes down the file size of an image by eliminating redundancies in the data. GIF

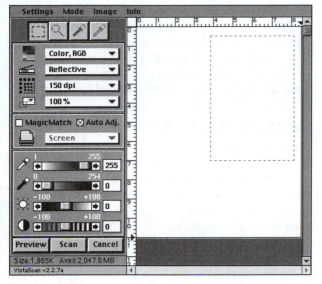

FIGURE 4.3 Scanner controls

images have the file ending **.gif**. GIF is the preferred format for images with sharp lines, buttons with text, visual icons, and other small images. GIF uses a "no loss" compression format, which means that all the information in the image is maintained. But the GIF format often makes photographic images splotchy. Thus GIF images are good for icons with sharp lines and solid colors, but not so good for large photographs and complex images. When you save a GIF image in Photoshop, you will need first to open the Mode menu and select Indexed color rather than RGB.

JPEG images

JPEG is an acronym for Joint Photographic Experts Group, and, as the name suggests, is the preferred format for photographs when people want the best photographic quality possible. JPEG images have file names ending **.jpeg** or **.jpg**. JPEG compresses the data in a photograph and rearranges it so that it tends to blend the colors but loses some of the detail. For this reason it is not suited for fine text, which it makes look blurry. JPEG compression can be increased to reduce the size of a file as much as 100 times smaller than the original. But as the compression increases, the quality decreases, so at some point you have to decide which is more important— a fast download time or the quality of the image.

Using an image editor

The best way to learn how to use an image editor like Adobe Photoshop is to get a copy of the program and then work your way through the tutorials. What may appear complicated at first becomes much clearer when you see it on the screen. Photoshop allows you to build an image in layers, so that you can design a Web page by focusing on a few elements at a time. It keeps track of the changes you make, so you can go back to an earlier stage if you don't like what you've just done. If you don't have access to Photoshop and don't want to buy it, you can find shareware programs on the Web that allow you to do some simple image editing including Picture Man (for Windows) and GraphicConverter (for Macintosh).

Whatever editor you use, there are a few manipulations that you will need to use frequently. It's always a good idea to copy the image first and work on the copy.

- **Cropping.** Most images can be trimmed, which gives them better visual focus and smaller file size. To crop an image, select the rectangle tool, draw the rectangle over the area you want to keep, and select the Crop or Trim command. The part of the image outside the rectangle will be discarded. Every pixel you can squeeze out makes it appear faster on a user's screen.
- **Sizing images.** Web editors allow you to declare the size of an image, and you should use the HEIGHT and WIDTH to give the dimensions of each image. Images load faster when you provide the dimensions, and it gives you some control

over how they will appear. You can give either exact dimensions in pixels or you can set the attribute by percentage. Web editors allow you to give custom size dimensions, and you can also go into the source HTML file and make adjustments. Suppose, for example, you have a banner image that you want to go all the way across the user's page, no matter how big or little their screen size. If you open up the HTML file, you can add a WIDTH command that tells the browser to extend the image from one side to the other, no matter how many pixels the screen can display:

```
<IMG SRC="banner.gif" WIDTH="100%">
```

- **Resizing.** All editors will give you the height and width of an image, which you should insert as attributes to the <IMG> tag. In addition, you can resize images to fit in a particular area of a Web page. If you have several images to display (for example, on a page of your photographs), you might consider making clickable thumbnail images that would link to full size images on separate pages. You should always check the resolution and bring it down to 72 dpi if needed.
- **Adjusting colors.** Often the colors in photographs that you scan appear off when you view the image on a computer monitor. Sometimes the image is too dark and needs brightening. Sometimes it doesn't have enough contrast. Sometimes the mix of red, green, and blue isn't right and you have to correct it. The basic controls for brightness, contrast, and color saturation are similar to those on your color TV.
- **Making part of a GIF image transparent.** You can declare a single color of a GIF image as transparent. This utility is quite useful for making buttons and other icons that appear to float over the background. However, if the background color of the image does not match the background color where you place the GIF on your Web page, an

ugly halo effect sometimes will surround the GIF. If you are working with Photoshop to create the GIF, use the eyedropper tool to sample the background color from where you are going to place the transparent GIF. Use that color for the background on the bottom layer and put the image on an overlying layer. Then you can save the GIF file and place it on your page.

Colors on Macintosh and Windows

Different browsers on different platforms do not display colors the same way. A GIF image with solid colors may look great on a Macintosh but bad on Windows. The full 8-bit color palette has 256 colors, but only 216 are shared by Macintosh and Windows. The other 40 colors will *dither*, which makes colors look speckled. If you want to be sure your images look good on all platforms, you should use the 216 Web-safe colors that display the same across platforms. On Photoshop 5.0 you can select the Web color palette, which includes the Web-safe colors. The Web-safe color palette is also available on the Web so you can copy it and sample colors from it.

Background images

Background images can be added to your page with any Web page editor or with the BACKGROUND attribute in the BODY tag <BODY BACKGROUND= "notebook.gif">. Background images are usually small GIF files that repeat without creating seams. Simple backgrounds are much preferred.

One of the most popular background image patterns is the notebook page.

It's also one of the easiest to read.

Elaborate background images distract from the central content, make text hard to read, and slow down the loading of a Web page. A 60K background image could add 30 seconds to the load time, which is unacceptable to many users. Keep any background images small, no more than 4K.

Use tables effectively

When graphic designers trained for print first moved to the Web, they quickly became frustrated. They found they could not control some of the most basic design features such as line length. The length of a line of text, which is a critical factor for readability, depended on how wide the user made the browser window—narrow windows meant short line lengths; wide windows created long lines.

Clever designers wanted control of page layout and soon began adapting tools for this purpose. One of the most powerful tools HTML offers for page layout is inserting tables. All Web page editors and most word processing programs allow you to create tables with similar commands (see Figure 4.4).

1. In Composer, select the table icon on the Composition Toolbar (or select **Table** on the **Insert** menu).
2. Specify the number of horizontal rows and vertical columns in the Table Properties dialog box.
3. Specify the table width in percentage.

You can also select the alignment (left, right, or center), the width of the table border, the spacing between cells, and the padding within cells. The dialog box in Figure 4.4 produces the table below:

Column 1	Column 2
Item 1A	Item 2A
Item 1B	Item 2B

Tables are valuable for presenting schedules, spreadsheets, price lists, comparative data, and other information that lends itself to this format. But they have many other uses besides making conventional tables, including aligning text and images on a page. They also allow you to create two- and three-column formats (see Figure 4.5).

Tables are also straightforward to hand code. You declare the boundaries of the table with a pair of tags <TABLE> and </TABLE>. Then you declare a table row <TR> that contains a cell of table data <TD>. A <TD> cell is the equivalent of a column. Inside that column you can create a "nested" table that will subdivide that column. Using tables can give you lots of white space and allows precise positioning of individual elements. When you use tables for layout, be sure to set the border to 0.

Formatting a text with style sheets

A major drawback of using tables for layout lies in creating difficulties for visually impaired users who rely on speech synthesis. The visually impaired user

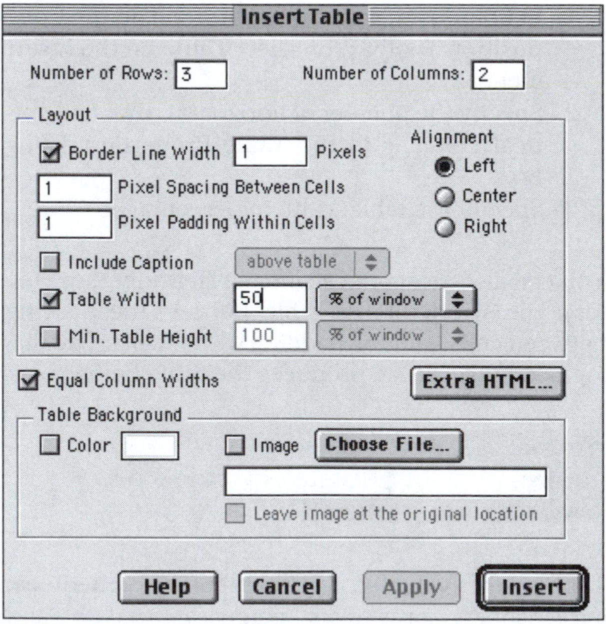

FIGURE 4.4 Table dialog box in Composer

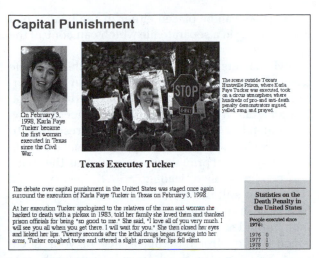

Capital Punishment

On February 3, 1998, Karla Faye Tucker became the first woman executed in Texas since the Civil War.

The scene outside Texas Huntsville Prison, where Karla Faye Tucker was executed, took on a circus atmosphere where hundreds of pro- and anti-death penalty demonstrators argued, yelled, sang and prayed.

Texas Executes Tucker

The debate over capital punishment in the United States was staged once again surround the execution of Karla Faye Tucker in Texas on February 3, 1998.

At her execution Tucker apologized to the relatives of the man and woman she hacked to death with a pickax in 1983, told her family she loved them and thanked prison officials for being "so good to me." She said, "I love all of you very much. I will see you all when you get there. I will wait for you." She then closed her eyes and licked her lips. Twenty seconds after the lethal drugs began flowing into her arms, Tucker coughed twice and uttered a slight groan. Her lips fell silent.

Statistics on the Death Penalty in the United States

People executed since **1976:**

1976	0
1977	1
1978	0

FIGURE 4.5   The use of tables for column layout

hears a lot of noise and text is often presented out of order. The long-term solution for layout on the Web is **style sheets,** which work much like those on your word processing program. Style sheets allow you to set defaults for elements such as fonts, colors, and headings, and they can control precise placement of images and other elements.

Similar to word processing programs, styles can apply to only a section of a document, the entire document, or a set of documents. The standard for style sheets on the Web is **cascading style sheets or CSS.** The name "cascade" comes from how they work: the browser descends through author and user specifications to browser defaults. CSS is supported by all 4.0 and later versions of Netscape and Internet Explorer.

The simplest style rules associate a declaration with an HTML tag. For example, if you want all level 1 headings to be white on a red background and in Arial font or another sans serif font, you can declare the style like this:

H1 {color: white; background: red; font-style: Arial sans-serif;}

These rules can be placed either in the header of a document or in a separate file which can control the appearance of many pages.

Style sheets allow designers to achieve some effects that are difficult or impossible in older versions of HTML. High-end Web page editors (e.g., Macromedia Dreamweaver) use style sheets for layout and allow for precision without resorting to tables. Style sheets allow designers to make specifications typical of print documents such as the space between lines called "leading."

You can still use style sheets even if you don't have access to a high-end editor. The W3C consortium provides style sheets that you can link to, which will control the appearance of your document. You can view the different effects each style gives in advance. These prepackaged styles are linked off one of the W3C pages: (http://www.w3.org/StyleSheets/Core/). The HTML link to these style sheets, which you can paste into the head of your page, is also available on this site.

Design for Maximum Performance

Always keep in mind that many users cannot experience everything on the Web because their access is by telephone modem. If they have a 28.8 modem, it takes 15 seconds to load a Web page with 30K of information. When the user is sitting in front of a blank screen, 15 seconds can seem like an eternity. They may well give up, click on the stop button, and move on to another site. Or they may turn off the images and find there is nothing on the site but images—if the designer has not labeled them, the user has no clue about what's there.

The ALT attribute

Perhaps you don't care about users with telephone modem connections. Most Web designers, however, cannot be so casual about tossing out such a big

---

LEARNING CSS

MULDER'S STYLESHEETS TUTORIAL

**http://www.hotwired.com/webmonkey/
stylesheets/tutorials/tutorial1.html**

STYLESHEETS REFERENCE

**http://www.hotwired.com/webmonkey/
stylesheets/reference/**

CSS RESOURCES

http://www.w3.org/Style/css/

---

chunk of their potential viewers. Figure 4.6 is the home page of a major bank with the images turned off on a browser. What is this bank saying to customers who want to check their bank balances online using a slow connection? And what about customers who are blind or have poor vision and rely on speech synthesis of text?

It doesn't have to be this bad. At the very least, the designer should have provided alternate text attributes for the images on this page, which will supply text for users who have images turned off. Alternate text attributes are simple to insert into image tags; for example <IMG SRC="whale.jpg" ALT="humpback whale breaching">. After ALT=, you supply text inside quotes that describes the image that the user doesn't see.

Designing for screen size

You can design Web pages with images that nearly all users can access, including those with slow dial-up modem connections, if you take into account the sizes of your users' screens and the sizes of the pictures and graphics you put on your pages. Screen sizes vary widely, from 640 × 480 for many laptops and older computers up to 1600 × 1200 on newer monitors. You can expect most users to be clustered at the bottom end, with 640 × 480, 800 × 600, and 832 × 624 screens.

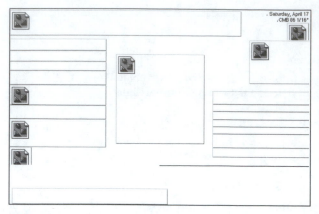

FIGURE 4.6　Web site of a major bank with images turned off

Professional Web designers attempt to stay within these dimensions. They are constantly aware that most users will not spend much time scrolling down a page.

Moreover, many users do not set their browsers to fill up the screen, and designers do not know how users set their preferences. Some users want larger type size and set their preferences accordingly, further reducing the amount of text that appears. Experienced designers know that it is what's up front that counts; they put the most important content in the first 300 pixels—roughly the top 60 percent of a 640 × 480 screen.

Accessible Design

In addition to those users with small screens and slow connections, many others may not be able to see, hear, move easily, or process some information easily. To reach the entire community of users, it is important to have text equivalents for any pictures, audio, or video you might put on your site. Any graphs or charts should have summaries attached. Visually impaired users have access to text through screen reader technology that reads the text aloud.

Including text equivalents has other advantages. Search engines that might otherwise miss your site have more words to identify when you describe an image with a text equivalent. Style sheets also greatly assist users with disabilities because they separate presentation from content. All users benefit from good navigation tools, which are discussed in the next chapter. Guidelines for accessibility are on the W3C site (http://www.w3.org/TR/1999/WAI-WEBCONTENT/).

The Center for Applied Special Technology (CAST) is committed to making the Web accessible to people with disabilities. CAST offers a Web-based tool called "Bobby" that analyzes Web pages for their accessibility to people with disabilities. You can submit your site to Bobby (http://www.cast .org/bobby/), which will tell you what potential problems it contains for people with disabilities, as well as any browser compatibility errors.

Building a Multi-Page Site

CHAPTER 5

Principles of Navigational Design

Print vs. Web navigation

When we look for something in a book, we rely on an elaborate set of navigational tools. At the most basic level, we know that books are continuous. If a sentence doesn't end on a particular page, we expect to find the remainder at the beginning of the next page. Books we use to find information are divided into chapters, which in turn are often divided into sections with headings. They have elaborate tables of contents and detailed indexes that give us specific page references, which we use to access specific information. When books are collected in a library, we rely on well developed tools that allow us to locate a particular book. These tools seem so natural to use that it's hard to imagine books and libraries without them. The navigational tools of print, however, including page numbers, titles and headings, chapters, tables of contents, indexes, and library classification systems, took centuries to develop.

Few people had heard of the Web before 1994; thus it's no wonder that Web navigational tools often seem so rudimentary. You do see some borrowing of print tools for Web navigation, but their adaptability is limited. The key difference is that navigational tools for print are based on book technology with continuously bound numbered pages. A Web site does not have to be sequential. Indeed, many sites are like a huge drawer stuffed full of odds and ends, and your job is to try to arrange what's in the drawer.

Organizing a Web site

How then do you begin? Many multi-page Web sites use a tree structure that spreads outward like the branches of a tree. That solution works reasonably well for many subjects, but what happens when you want to get from one side of the tree to the other? Do you have to retrace your path back to the trunk of the tree and then start down another branch? Many users don't want to do that much clicking. Designing a multi-page Web site presents many conceptual and design problems, but like visual design, there are a few basic principles that can provide solutions for many of these problems.

Make the navigational structure intuitive

The best navigational structures allow users to do what comes naturally. For example, on a Web site with pages in a linear sequence, users expect to be able to move forward and backward easily. Users also expect to find what they are looking for, so you should anticipate their needs. Suppose you are designing a Web site for your club or organization. Think first about who will be likely to visit the site. Some people will be curious to know what the club does, so you will need an "about" page. Some may want to join, so it should be easy to find out how. Members of your club will want to know about activities. They should have an obvious path to that information.

Make the navigational structure visible

How to move through a Web site should be evident from the beginning. An overview of your site should be presented in the navigational tools on the first page. The tools should reflect the primary subjects of your site.

Make the navigational structure consistent

The format of the navigational tools should be kept consistent from one page to another. For example, if your main navigational tool is a row of buttons down the left side on the page, you should stick with that design. Colors used for navigation should also remain consistent.

Keep the user oriented

Visitors to your site should always know where they are on your site. The navigational tools should indicate where the user is located on a site and should provide a clear path back to the beginning. Users should not have to resort to the back button on the browser.

Provide limited options at any given point

On a Web site of 10 to 15 pages, a user is not likely to feel overwhelmed. But when sites grow larger and many choices are offered at a single point, a user can feel overwhelmed if the choices are not grouped. That's when you have to make some hard decisions about your main menu items.

Tools for Navigation

Just as the basic unit of computing is a binary number or bit, the link is the basic navigational tool on the Web. A multi-page Web site without links is like a pizza without cheese—the key ingredient is missing. You have several ways of placing links on your site.

Embedded links

The simplest method of putting links on your site is to make a link off words in your text.

1. Click on the link icon or select **Link** on your Web page editor.
2. Highlight or type in the word or words you want to use for the link.
3. Type in the URL for where you want the link to go.
4. Click OK, and you've got a link.

You can create links quickly using this method, but there are disadvantages. You don't create a navigational structure for your site and you don't keep users oriented to their location on your site. Embedded links are useful, but you need additional navigational tools for a multi-page site.

Images as links

You can make an image serve as a link just as for text. In Chapter 2, Rachel Jones's home page was presented as an example. Suppose she has another page about humpback whales in a file named humpback.html that she wants to link to the image of the whale on her home page. In Composer she clicks on the insert image icon, types the file name whale.jpg in the Image File Name box, then clicks link, and types humpback.html in the URL or File box.

If Rachel coded by hand, the HTML code for the link would be:

```
<A HREF="humpback.html">
<IMG SRC="whale.jpg"
ALT="humpback whale" WIDTH=295
HEIGHT=195
BORDER ="0"></A>
```

Making an image into a link automatically inserts a 2-pixel-wide blue line surrounding the image. To remove the line, specify BORDER ="0".

Text navigation bars

One of the easiest navigational tools to create is a text bar with links, such as:

Home | My Courses | My Hobbies | Photos | Links

You can copy this code, open the other pages, and paste in the navigation bar. When you make it once, you don't have to make it again. On long pages, even if you have navigational tools at the top, a simple text bar at the bottom saves your visitor from having to scroll back up.

Buttons and icons

Creating a set of navigation buttons is almost as easy as making a text navigation bar. Buttons with or without text can be created quickly in Photoshop and other image editors. Editors have a text tool that allows you to type on a button image, which you can then save as a GIF file. Then you make the image file into a link to wherever you want users to go when they click the button. You can also insert text beside the button. Many clip art sites on the Web and clip art files included with software provide you with ready-to-use buttons. Buttons, icons, and images can add interest and humor to your site (see Figure 5.1).

FIGURE 5.1   Example of clip art

When you are designing a site that lends itself well to visual icons, you can use images organic to that site. Many art museums use representative images to provide visual guides. The home page of the Art Institute of Chicago uses thumbnails to represent its major collections (see Figure 5.2).

Image maps

If you have ever noticed the cursor changing into a pointing hand when you dragged it across an image, you were looking at an image map. The idea behind an image map is relatively simple; you define an area of an image and then attach a link to that area. Making the image map, however, is more complicated.

First, you need to find or create an image that provides a visual map. You should think carefully about how you can represent visually the structure of your site. If you have an image that lends itself well to division into clickable sections, such as a floor plan of a building where a user can click on different rooms, then half the work is done. Otherwise you have to create an image with distinct sections.

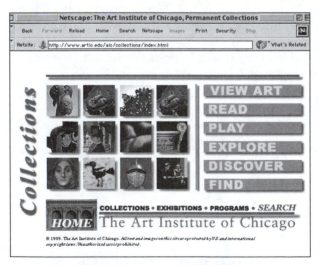

FIGURE 5.2 The Art Institute of Chicago, Permanent Collections (http://www.artic.edu/aic/collections/)

Second, you have to create the map that assigns links to different sections of the image. You define "hot spots" on the image so when a user clicks on that spot, the user will be taken to the URL that you specify for that spot (see Figure 5.3). Unless you are using an advanced Web page editor (e.g., Macromedia Dreamweaver), you will need to get a shareware image map program. You can find a list of free or demo image map programs on Yahoo (http://dir.yahoo.com/Computers_and_Internet/Internet/World_Wide_Web/Imagemaps/Software/).

Follow these steps to make an image map:

1. Open the image map program.
2. Open your HTML file and select the image you want to use for the image map if you have more than one on the page.
3. Type a name for the map in the Map Name dialog box.
4. Use the circle, square, or polygon tools to define hot spots on the image.
5. Type the URL for each hot spot in the Link dialog box.

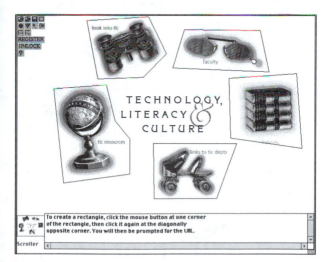

FIGURE 5.3 Defining hot spots using the shareware program Mapedit

6. When you have defined all of the hot spots, click OK.

Always provide an alternative for users who have their images turned off. For example, the home page for the Concentration in Technology, Literacy, and Culture includes a text navigation bar below the image map (see Figure 5.4).

Linking within the same page

If you have long pages of text that require scrolling down more than two windows, you should create links to move around on that page. These intrapage links are called **Targets** or **Anchors.** Composer and other editors allow you to create targets. On Composer, follow these steps:

1. Put the cursor at the beginning of a line or select some text.
2. Select **Target** on the **Insert** menu.
3. Type in a name for the target in the edit box or you will see the text that you selected.

FIGURE 5.4 Home page for the Concentration in Technology, Literacy, and Culture (http://www.tlc.utexas.edu)

4. Click OK. You will see a target icon in the Composer window where you marked the text.
5. Select the text or image that you want to link to the target.
6. Select **Link** on the **Insert** menu.
7. Select **Browse Page** on the **File** menu and click the link you just made.

Using Frames

Frames allow you to create windows within windows. Each frame in a browser window operates independently and has its own URL. Frames allow you to have fixed components on your site that stay visible when a user links to other pages on or off the site. Otherwise, when you provide links off your site, users have to use the Back button to return to your site.

The major disadvantage of using frames is that because they divide up screen real estate they can make it hard for users to display anything adequately. Frame borders create clutter if they are not turned off. When frames are too small, users have to do a lot of scrolling to see what's on a page—something that many users refuse to do. Another problem occurs when you link to another site with frames, which results in frames within frames. The current trend is moving away from using frames.

Creating frames

Not all Web editors allow you to create frames. They can be hand coded, and the process is not difficult with a basic knowledge of HTML (a good tutorial on coding frames is at: http://junior.apk.net/~jbarta/frames.html). Editors that allow you to create frames make it much easier. Under the **Edit** menu on Adobe PageMill you can find commands for **Split Horizontally** and **Split Vertically** that create separate windows (see Figure 5.5).

You will probably want to keep one window for your navigational tools. The navigation window

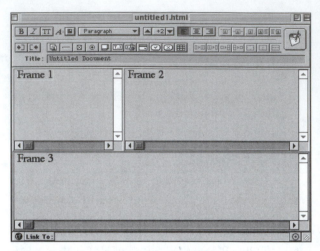

FIGURE 5.5   Frames on Adobe PageMill

should not require scrolling. Also make sure that any images you include fit within the window where you insert them. Keep some space around the images. Finally, test your frame site with different browsers on different platforms to make sure that users see what you intend.

Navigation on Complex Sites

Most class projects lend themselves to straightforward navigational schemes because they have fewer than twenty pages. But you may become involved in designing a more complex site for an organization you belong to or for an employer or even for yourself. Often when Web sites grow, they end up serving several different functions. When the mission of a site becomes complex, the navigational tools should reflect that complexity rather than lumping everything together in one chaotic list of links.

The welcome page for the Longman Web site, the publisher of this book, has five main items on the image map in the center with a text navigation bar below (see Figure 5.6). On the left side, it offers a

FIGURE 5.6 Welcome page for Longman
(http://www.awlonline.com/longman/)

link for instructors who wish to examine books, as
well as general links and a link for prospective
authors. On the right side, the disciplines in which
Longman publishes are listed, so a user can quickly
find the Longman titles in particular areas.

The "bread crumb trail" approach

If you are putting up page after page on a deep site,
you should always be sure to make it easy for the
user to get back to the preceding page. Users should
always be able to retrace their steps without having
to click on the Back button. If you have long pages
with the navigational tools on the top, then you
should put in an anchor that returns the user to the
top of the page.

Creating a Dynamic Web Site

CHAPTER 6

Interacting with People on the Web

You now have everything you need for a Web site. You have content, visual design, and navigational tools, and it's all up on the Web for the world to see. But there's more. Some of the most interesting—and most popular—sites on the Internet use a variety of techniques to make their pages more appealing and exciting. They engage visitors by giving them opportunities to interact and respond. This chapter will introduce you to the many possibilities of enhancing your Web site by taking advantage of the Web's capability for presenting audio, animation, and even video.

You don't have to have the full sound and light show, however, to interact with visitors to your Web site. One important feature of every Web page, even a basic one, is to have some method of response so that visitors can comment on the Web site they are viewing. As a general rule you should have your email address available somewhere on the page. By including your address, you do run a risk of receiving hostile email, but that risk is usually small. Compliments and topical comments from those interested in the subject of your site almost always outweigh any negative posts.

Putting an email link on your page

A simple way to facilitate interaction is to include an email link on your page. You can insert an HTML tag for an email to you, which looks like this:

```
<A HREF="mailto:nobody@somewhere.net">
Mail me!</A>
```

When you replace the nobody@somewhere.net with your own email address, visitors can send you email by clicking on Mail me! Many Web designers place this tag at the bottom of every page. A small addition can also supply a subject line to the message:

```
<A HREF="mailto:
nobody@somewhere.net?subject=webpages">
Mail me!</A>
```

The ?subject=webpages after your email address will automatically make the subject of the email whatever you type after subject=.

Including CGI scripts and forms on your page

CGI, an acronym for "Common Gateway Interface," allows users to run programs on a host computer, creating Web pages on the fly and immediately sending them out to the user. The remarkable power of search engines is made possible by CGI but that's only one example. CGI scripts do many other things from managing chat rooms to informing you of your checking account balance to controlling robotic arms remotely.

Most CGI scripts are written in the Perl programming language, though other programming languages such as C/C++, Visual Basic, AppleScript, and UNIX Shell are also used. Perl is the language of choice because it is designed to access multiple text files and reformat them according to what the user wants. If you decide to include CGI on your page, you don't have to be a programmer. Many CGI scripts are available for free on the Web, including scripts that set up interactive event calendars, guestbooks, Web-based bulletin boards, clocks, and the counters that you see on so many Web pages. Scripts can be found at http://worldwidemart .com/scripts/ or at http://www.extropia.com/prod ucts.html, as well as other places on the Web.

You do, however, have to place the scripts on your server. Since CGI scripts are potentially dangerous security flaws in a computer system, check with the person in charge of the server you are using before running any scripts. The system operator will probably have some method specific to that computer for implementing scripts. Most often, you'll have to place all of your scripts in one directory, under public_html, called cgi-bin. You may be able to put the scripts in any directory, or you may have to submit the scripts to the systems operator for special placement in another directory. Installing CGI scripts involves some serious under-the-hood work, but fortunately, most of the scripts available on the Web come with extensive installation instructions. You need patience when dealing with CGI scripts. If it doesn't work right the first time, it's not hopeless. Often it takes massive tinkering, especially the first few times you deal with CGI, to get everything in place.

The script itself is nothing without the Web page on which a user enters information. These Web pages contain **forms;** if you have ever typed information on a Web page, you were almost certainly using a form of some sort. Forms are HTML code, and follow most of the same rules. A simple form that doesn't require a CGI script sends the information instead directly to an email address. In order to produce the Web page in Figure 6.1, place the following code in an HTML file (replace "youraddress@yourhost.edu" with your own email address, of course):

```
<FORM METHOD=POST ACTION="yourad
dress@yourhost.edu"
ENCTYPE="text/plain">
Subject:        <INPUT TYPE=TEXT NAME=SUB
JECT WIDTH=50><BR>
Message:     <BR><TEXTAREA NAME=BODY
ROWS=15 COLS=80></TEXTAREA>
<BR><INPUT TYPE=SUBMIT VALUE="send!">
</FORM>
```

You can find CGI scripts using Yahoo's CGI directory (http://dir.yahoo.com/Computers_and _Internet/Internet/World_Wide_Web/CGI_Common _Gateway_Interface/). In particular, on http://www .cgi-resources.com/, you can find a large set of links and information about CGI. An invaluable resource to learn more about CGIs and forms is http://junior .apk.net/~jbarta/tutor/forms/lesson01.html. Also, http://www.cgi-resources.com/Programs_and _Scripts/Remotely_Hosted/Form_Processing/ provides a list of scripts which are hosted remotely on other servers, saving you the trouble of putting them on your server.

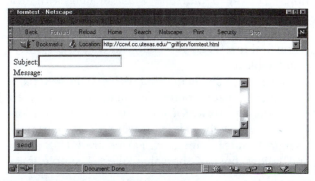

FIGURE 6.1 Example of a simple form created with HTML

Digital Audio

Many Web sites offer audio components in addition to their other content. Audio can come in a variety of forms, but the most common audio files on the Web are sampled sounds in various formats. Audio files can greatly enhance a site, but except for video, nothing requires more bandwidth. Many users will have to wait a long time for your sound files to download, so you should make sure that their wait is going to be worth it.

Capturing and editing audio files

Audio files were developed to be played on specific hardware, and thus there are several different formats. The three most common types are:

1. AIFF (.aif, .aiff) for Macintosh
2. AU (.au) for UNIX Workstations
3. WAVE (.wav) for Windows

Current browsers have no difficulty with all these formats. Computers with sound cards installed usually come with some program that is able to record these files.

In Windows, for example, the Sound Recorder program, called sndrec.exe or sndrec32.exe depending on your version of Windows, can record WAVE files. When you open the Sound Recorder program, you will get a control panel:

Press the red record button on the right to begin recording from the microphone. (You might need to buy a microphone if your computer did not come with one. Check your sound card manual for details.)

You can also use audio files that you have saved on your computer. Remember that they must be in either WAVE, AU, or AIFF to be played on most browsers. Most sound editing software will allow you to convert other audio formats into one of these three. If a sound editing program did not come with your sound card, there are shareware programs available on the Web. Again, Yahoo is a good place to start when looking for shareware and demo software that you can use for a limited time (http://dir.yahoo.com/Computers_and_Internet/Software/Multimedia/Audio/).

Sound editing software can also be useful to add interesting effects, such as doppler, distortion, echo, and pitch. Goldwave, a shareware digital audio editor for Windows, can be used for CD editing as well as making sound files for Web pages. The controls in these programs resemble the buttons on a tape recorder, so they are not difficult to learn (see Figure 6.2).

Broadcast audio

A new format of audio files that has gained wide popularity is the MP3, or Mpeg-Layer III file, which produces a high-quality recording that uses very little space. A CD quality song can be as small as four megabytes, whereas a normal audio file for the same song would be ten times as large. These MP3s are currently traded, but sites such as www.shoutcast.com allow people to broadcast their personal collection or listen to other broadcasts.

Another format of song files is MIDI, an acronym for Musical Instrument Digital Interface. MIDI files were designed to allow computers to communicate with synthesizers, keyboards, and other digital instruments. They are very small and can sound dif-

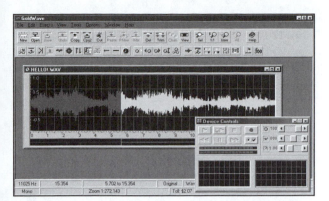

FIGURE 6.2 Controls for Goldwave, a shareware digital audio editor

ferent on different computers, as they only hold the notation and what instrument is playing. The computer then plays the appropriate digitized sound for each instrument, reconstructing the song. MIDIs are limited to instrumental-only songs. You can find MIDI files at many sites on the Web, or you can record your own. If you own a MIDI keyboard, you can play it and the computer can record directly. You should consult the manuals for your MIDI keyboard and your sound card for more information. You can also place the notes with your mouse in most MIDI recording programs.

If all these different sound file types are confusing, fortunately there is just one command for placing AIFF, AU, WAVE, and MIDI files on a Web page. First, they must be uploaded into the Web site. In the HTML file of the page that you want the sounds to be available on, put in this bit of HTML code:

```
<EMBED SCR="sound/background.mid"
HEIGHT=35 WIDTH=16 CONTROLLER=TRUE
AUTOPLAY=TRUE LOOP=TRUE>
```

This code will automatically start the file called background.mid in the sound directory. This could be a WAVE, AU, AIFF, MIDI, or, in fact, almost any kind of multi-media file—more on this later. If you do not want the file to repeat endlessly, replace loop=TRUE with loop=FALSE. By changing the height and width numbers, you change how large the controls for the sound will be. If you want to hide all controls and use the file as background sound only, replace controller=TRUE with controller=FALSE.

Streaming audio

The way of the future with audio on the Web is streaming audio. Streaming audio is recorded in a way that makes it easy for the computer to play the file while it is downloading the next part. The "streaming" metaphor is appropriate because it's like the difference between trying to empty an entire lake at once versus draining the lake through the gates of a dam. With the flow from a dam, eventually you will get all the water, just not all at once. Plus you don't have to wait for the entire lake to transfer before you get some water. In much the same way, you get to hear a streaming audio file as soon as the connection is made but before you get the entire file. Eventually you get it all.

RealAudio is the most common form of streaming audio. All the programs needed to produce this are available free at www.real.com. To create RealAudio (and RealVideo) you need RealProducer. This program takes input from files or your microphone and makes RealAudio files out of them. In fact, if you also download the free Basic Server from www.real.com and have a good connection to the Internet, you can broadcast your own live radio station from your computer.

When you open RealProducer, the program asks you to select the source of the audio (or video) that you wish to turn into a RealMedia file (see Figure 6.3).

Most often you will select "file" and browse to find the WAVE, AU, or AIFF file that you wish to encode. You could also click on Media Device and select Capture Audio to record directly from your microphone or line-in. Before continuing, you will either name the file to save RealMedia or select Live Broadcast to broadcast what you are inputting.

After you choose your set of options, a recording dialog box will prompt you for more information (see Figure 6.4). On the top are the input and output windows. If you are recording video, the video will be visible in both windows. If you are recording sound only, it shows the default picture. On the left you can type in your name, the title of the clip, and copyright information. On the right are various options available to you. Make choices based on your intended audience but remember: making your song available to everyone who visits your page may be more important than having a select few able to hear it very well. At the bottom of this window are various controls for the actual recording of the clip and some options on publishing it.

RealAudio allows you to include long sound files that users can hear as the files are downloading. Most servers have some form of RealAudio server available on them. To find out how to set up RealAudio, contact the administrator for the computer that your Web page is on. In general, you will

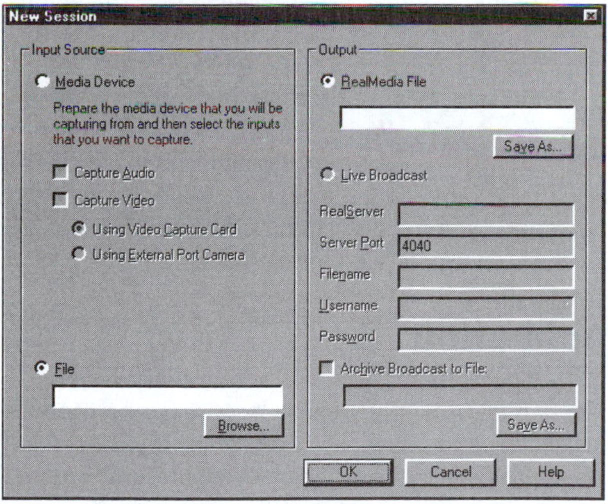

FIGURE 6.3 First screen of RealProducer

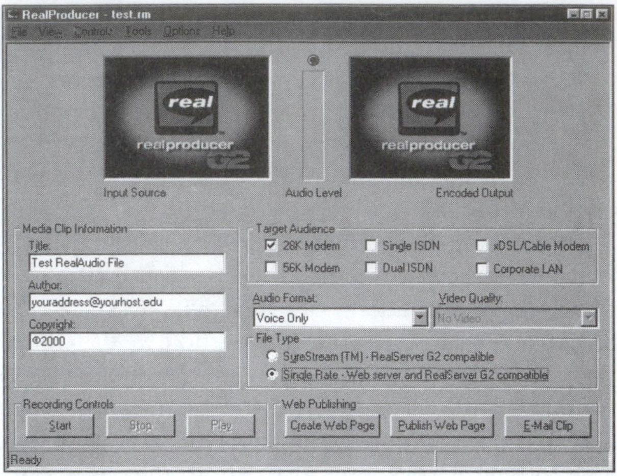

FIGURE 6.4   Dialog box for encoding audio files in RealProducer

have to place the RealAudio file in a specific directory on the host. Your Web page will link to what is called a **metafile,** which contains links to the actual RealMedia files. The Web Publishing options in the Producer can help you create a metafile. Again, many of these details are specific to how the administrator has set up the Web server, so look through help files or ask the administrator for help if you do not know how RealMedia is handled on your server.

Even if your Web server does not support RealAudio broadcasts, you might try some of the free Web page sites available, such as www.tripod.com, which allow RealAudio broadcasts and give you an ample amount of space.

Animation

Most animations on the Internet are in one of three forms: GIF animation, Shockwave, or Java. The simplest and cheapest animation available is GIF animation, and for these reasons GIF animation will be the focus of this chapter. Shockwave and Java offer game-quality animation, and while they are beyond the scope of this book, you'll find out how to learn more about them.

GIF Animation

Traditional animation requires making small changes in a series of images so that when they are viewed in rapid succession, they present the illusion of movement. Animated GIF files use this traditional method of making small changes in a series of images. If the image is kept small, a series of images load fast enough to give the animation effect. Almost all of the animated banner advertisements and small animations you see on Web pages are GIF files. GIF animation can enhance the appearance of your Web site, but the effect can be overdone easily. Animated GIFs draw attention to themselves, so if they are not used correctly, they can interfere with easy navigation of your page. They also can take a long time to load, so be aware if your intended users have dial-up modems.

Many archives of animated GIF files can be found on the Web, some of which you can use freely and thus do not have to create your own. Most of the easy animation possibilities, from bouncing balls to dancing hamsters, have already been done. You can copy an animation just as you can copy an image file by clicking on the animation (right click on Windows, or hold down the mouse button on Macintosh) and saving the image to your own disk. But be sure to ask permission before using the animation on your site. Many archives ask you to provide a link to them if you use their images. It's always polite to acknowledge your source, even when the copyright is waived.

Creating your own animations

Some projects will require a specific appearance, and you can create your own animations, tailored to your exact needs. GIF animations are nothing more than a series of images all saved in one file with a few instructions on how they should appear. To create a GIF animation, then, you will need an image manipulation program that can save GIF files. Adobe's Photoshop has an excellent "Export to GIF89a" option, and most image editors have similar options. A word of warning about GIF files before we go on. Animated or transparent GIF files are *always* GIF89a files. GIF87 is an earlier version that does not support these features. Most programs by default save the 89a version, but if you are given a choice, do *not* use the 87 version.

There are many basic GIF animators available for you to use as shareware or in demo versions, which will often be enough for one project. Shareware programs contain all the commands you need to make GIF animations, but you have to supply the images from elsewhere. Consequently, you should have a separate image editor such as Photoshop.

What's most fun about creating your own GIF animations is that you use the process of classic animation, drawing one animation frame after another, except it's a lot easier than drawing each frame from scratch. You can make an exact copy of any animation frame on the computer using the Save As command and modify only the section you want to make appear to move. Also, it's very simple to erase your mistakes with Control-Z (Windows) or Command-Z (Mac). Photoshop gives a history of each thing you do, making it easy to go back to an earlier stage. Of course, you can also copy and paste parts of images. Photographs are difficult to animate because they require huge files. Sketches and line art work better. Many people create GIF animations the old-fashioned way by drawing them in pencil and then scanning the drawings.

When you have a few animation frames ready, it's time to open your GIF animation program and start adding your frames. Popular shareware programs for creating GIF animations are Gif Construction Set (http://www.mindworkshop.com/alchemy/gifcon

.html) for Windows users and GifBuilder (http://iawww.epfl.ch/Staff/Yves.Piguet/clip2gif-home/GifBuilder.html) for Macintosh users.

Commands on a GIF animation program

Animated GIFs have six types of "blocks," or instructions: Header, Loop, Image, Plain Text, Control, and Comment. Figure 6.5 shows the sequence of commands for a simple animated banner, using the shareware program GIF Construction Set.

The **Header** block is usually automatically created by the animation program. It contains information about the size of the canvas that the animation frames will be placed on (which should match the size of the animation frames), and information about the colors, including the background color for the canvas.

The **Loop** block comes right after the Header block and does what its name suggests. It has one variable—iterations—which governs how many times the entire animation repeats.

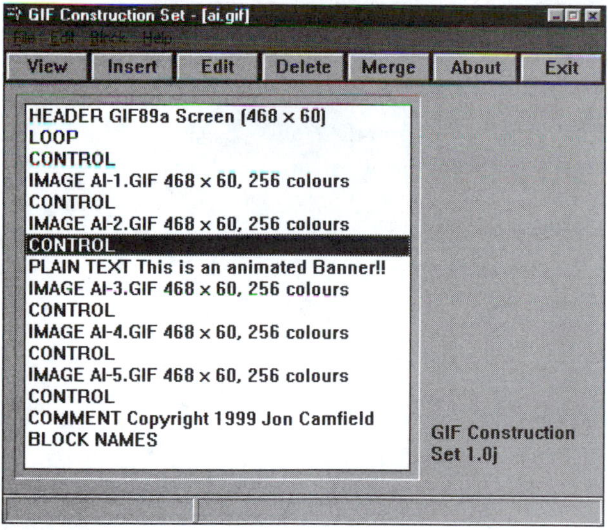

FIGURE 6.5 GIF Constuction Set

Image blocks hold the individual frames of animation, each of which is a plain GIF file. When you load an animation frame in the Image block, GIF Construction Set allows you to control where on the canvas the image appears, to assign colors individual to that frame (called the "palette"), and to interlace the image (interlaced images blur into view rather than appearing line by line). These commands are on the Image block editor (see Figure 6.6).

Plain Text blocks appear with the rest of the frames of animation. They are not often used, but they can reduce the file size if you are using a graphic to display text.

Control blocks are the most difficult blocks to deal with. You should have a Control block for each frame you have in your animation. Control blocks govern how long the next frame will stay on screen, what happens with the frame when it is through, whether it has transparent elements, and whether it must be clicked to move on. It is important to remember that Control blocks always affect the ani-

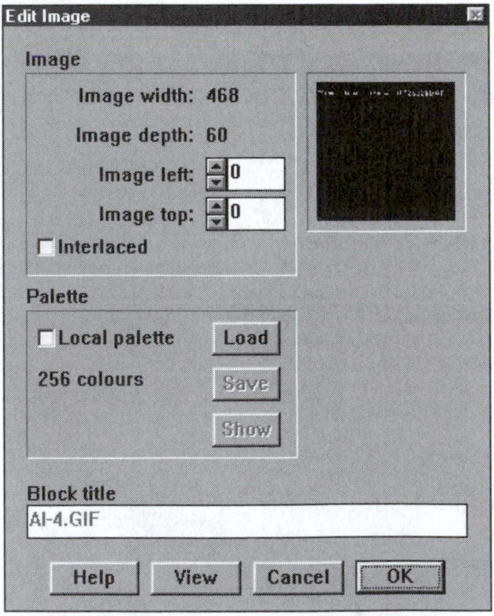

FIGURE 6.6 Image block editor on GIF Constuction Set

mation frame that they *precede*. The Control block editor from GIF Construction Set gives you these commands (see Figure 6.7).

If you designed a GIF with transparent areas, you will want to tell the GIF animator which color is the transparent one in this block. You can directly select the color entry if you know it, or, as is more common, use the eyedropper tool to select the color from the frame. The "Wait for user input" option is rarely used and not necessarily supported, but will stop the images from progressing until the user has pressed a key or clicked the mouse when it is supported. "Delay" is the measure of how long the frame stays fully visible before the next frame is loaded. Notice that this program measures delay in hundredths of a second!

Finally, the **Comment** block allows you to put in information that is *not* seen by the end-user. These blocks are often used for copyright and creation date information, or notes on how the image was created.

Creating an animation with GIF Construction Set

When you have your animation frames ready, you can create an animation with GIF Construction Set. Make sure that all the animation frames are the same height and width, and then follow these steps:

1. Select **New** from the **File** menu.
2. Click on **Insert** and select **Loop**.
3. Click on **Insert** again and select **Control block**. Set the delay to 1/100th of a second.
4. Click on **Insert** again and add the first animation frame.
5. Repeat steps 3 and 4 until all frames are added.
6. Open the **Header** block and make sure the height and width matches the size of your frames.
7. Save your file.

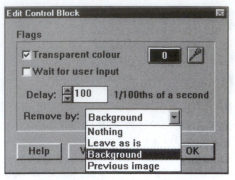

FIGURE 6.7 Control block editor on GIF Construction Set

Macromedia Shockwave

Macromedia Director is the most popular authoring software for making multimedia presentations on both Windows and Macintosh systems, including CD-ROMs and interactive movies. Director has tools that allow you to combine graphics, sound, animation, text, and video in one presentation. Shockwave is the technology that allows these presentations to be viewed on Web pages. The plug-in for Shockwave is now part of the package you get when you download Netscape, Internet Explorer, or AOL. Learning how to make presentations in Shockwave requires a major time commitment, and unless you have access to Director in a computer lab, the software will also cost you quite a few dollars. But if you want to become a serious Web designer, both investments are well worth it. The Macromedia Web site (http://www.macromedia.com) has a lot of information about Director and Flash, another powerful multimedia technology.

Java

Unlike the other applications discussed in this book, Java is a programming language that takes a significant commitment to learn. Nonetheless, you'll come into frequent contact with Java if you spend much time on the Web. Most of the interest in Java centers on applets, which are miniature programs that perform one function on a larger Web page. The advantage of applets is that they allow a user's computer to generate some of what would otherwise have to be sent over the Internet. They permit much faster loading of certain parts of a Web page and thus can make the user's experience more highly interactive. Java is used often for Web animations and easy-to-use interfaces. Java is complicated, but like CGI, Java applets are available on the Web for you to install and use. The creator of Java, Sun Microsystems, has an extensive Web site that describes how to learn Java (http://www.javasoft.com).

Digital Video

The creation of digital video is similar to digital audio. You need to record the video with a video camera or have some video already shot (a VHS tape). You then need some way to get this information into the computer (a video capture card or similar technology). Finally, you need a program (e.g., Adobe Premiere) to edit video files and convert them into a format (e.g., QuickTime) that a Web browser can recognize and display on both Windows and Macintosh platforms. If you buy everything you need, you will pay from a few hundred to a few thousand dollars, so check with your school first to see if you can get access to any or all of these devices and software.

Video file sizes are enormous, and they must be compressed to be broadcast on the Web, then decompressed by the receiving computer. Information is lost in this process of compression and decompression; fine detail will be lost in most cases, and dark areas especially will be less detailed. Start with the highest quality video possible; low quality input will mean even lower quality output. After you have the video, set up your video capture card (preferably, get a computer lab technician to help you) and transfer the VHS to digital format. Alternatively, you can use a digital video camera to record directly to computer media. These come in a variety of types and costs. Cameras which are not mobile (they are attached directly to your computer) are cheaper, but you have to be in reach of your computer at all times when recording. Digital video cameras which record to a disk are currently very expensive, but if you have access to one, you don't have to pay for a separate video capture card.

The next step is to use a digital video editor (e.g., Adobe Premiere) to make your video. Before you begin this process, it's critical to analyze your potential audience. If you are aiming only for campus users with high-speed connections, you can go for higher quality. But if you want modem users to see your video, you will need to know every trick in the book to reduce the file size to the lowest acceptable level. Adobe Premiere will ask you to specify frame size, frame rate, and data rate when you begin editing. Only high-end users will be able to view a 640×480 frame; more common is 160×120 (remember to add 20 pixels to the top of a QuickTime file for the controls). Likewise, you'll want to go with the slowest frame rate you can get by with—probably 12.5 or 10 frames per second.

The fun part is putting together the video. Adobe Premiere displays each frame on a Timeline (see Figure 6.8). You can trim and combine video clips just like the Hollywood professionals do, inserting transitions and adding sound. The Preview command allows you to view your work as soon as you

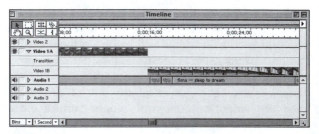

FIGURE 6.8   Timeline on Adobe Premiere

save the file. Premiere allows you to save your file in different formats including QuickTime (.mov).

You can place your QuickTime files on your Web server or you can convert them into RealMedia (.rm), which is proprietary software that drops the quality but allows modem users to see video. RealMedia video files are created exactly like RealAudio files. You have the input file in a format RealProducer can read (.mov or .avi), and RealProducer translates it into a RealMedia file (see Figure 6.9). You can already see the blurring in the "Encoded Output" window. For Internet broadcasting, this blurring and choppiness is inevitable.

When you have the video file, placing it on the Internet is almost exactly the same as with audio files. With QuickTime or avi movies, you use the command:

```
<EMBED SCR="path/to/file.mov" HEIGHT=180
WIDTH=120>
```

With RealMedia files, like RealAudio files, you should contact your system administrator for the details of how to put your files on the server. Like

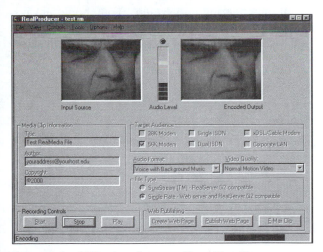

Figure 6.9 Dialog box for encoding video files on RealProducer

RealAudio, you will have an HTML file and a metafile. In the HTML file, you provide a path to the RealVideo metafile:

```
<A HREF="path/to/file.ram">Click here</A>
```

In the metafile, you provide a path to your RealVideo file:

```
pnm://realaudio.cc.utexas.edu/pat/to/file.rm
```

The Last Word on Design

The top Web designers will all tell you the same thing. Good design is not about doing everything the technology allows you to do—or, in their words, it's not about bells and whistles. Clear, effective communication succeeds on the Web just as it does in print. The most successful design is often not what draws attention to itself but what goes unnoticed.

You should also remember that many users will not be able to see the animations and video or hear the audio because they don't have the latest browser with a fast connection or because they have poor vision or a hearing impairment. You should always provide a text equivalent for any non-text media. Text is accessible to everyone through synthesized speech, braille, or visual display.

Web Sites in the Disciplines

Using Web Resources

More and more disciplinary resources are being placed on the Web. You can expect to find major library databases, government resources, sites of major professional organizations, links to online discussion groups, full text journals, electronic texts, teaching resources, case studies, and directories of schools and departments. Several libraries now have extensive lists of links to particular disciplines, including:

- **Infosurf**
  http://www.library.ucsb.edu/subj/resource.html
- **Internet Public Library**
  http://www.ipl.org/ref/RR/
- **Library of Congress Subject Guide**
  http://lcweb.loc.gov/global/subject.html
- **New York Public Library Resource Guides**
  http://www.nypl.org/admin/genweb/guides.html
- **Rice University Internet Guide**
  http://www.rice.edu/Fondren/Netguides/netguides.html

- **University of Alberta Subject Guide**
  http://www.library.ualberta.ca/library_html/
  subjects/index.html
- **University of Virginia Subject Guides**
  http://www.lib.virginia.edu/resguide.html
- **University of Waterloo Electronic Library Resources**
  http://www.lib.uwaterloo.ca/discipline/
  discip.html
- **Yale University Subject Guides**
  http://www.library.yale.edu/Internet/yalesir.html

Below is a selected list of important directories of Web resources listed by discipline. They are good places to start when exploring what is available on the Web in particular disciplines.

Humanities, Arts, and Architecture

Architecture and Building: Net Resources
- **Museums in the USA**
  http://library.nevada.edu/arch/rsrce/webrsrce/
  contents.html

Art and Art History
- **Art History Research Centre**
  http://www-fofa.concordia.ca/arth/AHRC/
  index.htm
- **Art History Resources on the Web**
  http://witcombe.sbc.edu/ARTHLinks.html
- **Museums in the USA**
  http://www.museumca.org/usa/
- **The Parthenet**
  http://home.mtholyoke.edu/~klconner/
  parthenet.html/
- **World Art Treasures**
  http://sgwww.epfl.ch/BERGER/

Classical Studies

- **Ancient World Web**
  http://www.julen.net/aw/
- **Library of Congress Classics Collection**
  http://lcweb.loc.gov/global/classics/classics
  .html

English and Foreign Languages

- **The English Server**
  http://english-server.hss.cmu.edu/
- **Modern Language Association of America**
  http://www.mla.org/
- **National Council of Teachers of English**
  http://www.ncte.org/
- **Project Gutenberg (online books)**
  http://promo.net/pg/

Film Studies

- **Internet Movie Database**
  http://us.imdb.com/

History

- **Indexes of Resources for History**
  http://history.cc.ukans.edu/history/
- **Library of Congress American Memory Project**
  http://lcweb2.loc.gov/amhome.html

Linguistics

- **Voice of the Shuttle Linguistics Page**
  http://humanitas.ucsb.edu/shuttle/hilights
  .html#linguistics

Philosophy

- **The American Philosophical Association**
  http://www.oxy.edu/apa/apa.html
- **Voice of the Shuttle Philosophy Page**
  http://humanitas.ucsb.edu/shuttle/philo.html

Rhetoric

- **Rhetoric and Argumentation Sites**
  http://www.drc.utexas.edu/stures/index.cfm
- **Rhetoric Resources at Georgia Tech**
  http://www.lcc.gatech.edu/gallery/rhetoric/
- **Rhetoric Server, University of California, Berkeley**
  http://rhetoric.berkeley.edu/

Women's Studies

- **New York Public Library Women's Studies Guide**
  http://www.nypl.org/research/chss/grd/resguides/
  women.html/
- **WSSLINKS: Women and Gender Studies Web Sites**
  http://www.library.yale.edu/wss/

Social Sciences, Education, and Law

Anthropology

- **UCSB Anthropology Web**
  http://www.anth.ucsb.edu/netinfo.html

Communication

- **Communication Resources, University of Iowa**
  http://www.uiowa.edu/~commstud/resources/
  index.html
- **CCMS Infobase**
  http://www.cultsock.ndirect.co.uk/MUHome/
  cshtml/
- **Media and Communication Studies site, University of Wales**
  http://www.aber.ac.uk/~dgc/medmenu.html

Economics

- **WebEc**
  http://netec.wustl.edu/WebEc/

Education

- **AskEric**
  http://ericir.syr.edu/
- **Educause**
  http://www.educause.edu/
- **Online Education WWW Server**
  http://www.online.edu/
- **NASA's Online Educational Resources**
  http://quest.arc.nasa.gov/OER/ .

Government

- **Bureau of the Census**
  http://www.census.gov/
- **The Digital Daily**
  http://www.irs.ustreas.gov/basic/cover.html
- **Fedworld**
  http://www.fedworld.gov/
- **Library of Congress**
  http://lcweb.loc.gov/
- **Political Science Resources on the Web**
  http://www.lib.umich.edu/libhome/Documents
  .center/polisci.html/
- **THOMAS (guide to current congressional legislation)**
  http://thomas.loc.gov/

Law

- **ABA LAWlink**
  http://www.abanet.org/lawlink/home.html
- **FindLaw**
  http://www.findlaw.com/
- **Internet Legal Resource Guide**
  http://www.ilrg.com
- **Law Resources on the Internet**
  http://www.lawyernet.com/legal.htm

Psychology

- **PsychNET**
  http://www.apa.org/psychnet/

- **Psychology Virtual Library**
  http://www.clas.ufl.edu/users/gthursby/psi/
- **Social Psychology Network**
  http://www.wesleyan.edu/spn/

Social Science
- **Social Science Information Gateway**
  http://sosig.esrc.bris.ac.uk/
- **Social Sciences Virtual Library**
  http://www.clas.ufl.edu/users/gthursby/socsci/

Sociology
- **Princeton Sociology Links**
  http://www.princeton.edu/~sociolog/links.html
- **SocioWeb**
  http://www.socioweb.com/~markbl/socioweb/

Natural Sciences, Medicine, and Engineering

Astronomy
- **American Astronomical Society**
  http://www.aas.org/
- **AstroWeb**
  http://www.stsci.edu/astroweb/astronomy.html
- **The Nine Planets**
  http://www.seds.org/billa/tnp/nineplanets.html

Biology
- **Biotech**
  http://biotech.icmb.utexas.edu/
- **Cell and Molecular Biology Online**
  http://www.cellbio.com/
- **Marine Biology Web**
  http://life.bio.sunysb.edu/marinebio/mbweb
  .html

Chemistry

- **American Chemical Society's ACS Web**
  http://www.acs.org/
- **The Learning Matters of Chemistry**
  http://www.knowledgebydesign.com/tlmc/
  tlmc.html
- **Science Hypermedia**
  http://www.scimedia.com/

Computer Science

- **Computer Science Research Resources**
  http://www.cs.umd.edu/documents/CSresources
  .html

Engineering

- **American Institute of Chemical Engineers**
  http://www.aiche.org/
- **Cornell's Engineering Library**
  http://www.englib.cornell.edu/
- **Electrical Engineering, University of Washington**
  http://www.ee.washington.edu/eeca/
- **Engineering Information Village**
  http://hood2.ei.org/eivill/plsql/village.serve
  _page?p=1280
- **EINet/Galaxy Engineering and Technology**
  http://galaxy.einet.net/galaxy/Engineering-and-
  Technology.html
- **National Academy of Engineering**
  http://www.nae.edu/nae/nae.nsf/

Environment

- **Envirolink**
  http://envirolink.org/
- **International Institute for Sustainable Development**
  http://iisd1.iisd.ca/

Geography

- **Association of American Geographers**
  http://www.aag.org/

Geology

- **American Geological Institute**
  http://www.agiweb.org/
- **American Geophysical Union**
  http://earth.agu.org/kosmos/homepage.html
- **Geological Society of America**
  http://www.geosociety.org/index.htm
- **Geological Surveys and Natural Resources**
  http://www.lib.berkeley.edu/EART/surveys.html

Health Science

- **Martindale's Health Science Guide**
  http://www-sci.lib.uci.edu/HSG/HSGuide.html
- **National Institutes of Health**
  http://www.nih.gov/

Mathematics

- **Math Archives**
  http://archives.math.utk.edu
- **The Math Forum**
  http://forum.swarthmore.edu/

Medicine

- **Doctor's Guide to the Internet**
  http://www.pslgroup.com/docguide.htm
- **Medline Plus, National Library of Medicine**
  http://www.nlm.nih.gov/
- **Medscape**
  http://www.medscape.com/
- **MedWeb**
  http://WWW.MedWeb.Emory.Edu/MedWeb/

Natural History and Paleontology

- **The Museum of Paleontology, University of California, Berkeley**
  http://www.ucmp.berkeley.edu/
- **National Museum of Natural History, Smithsonian Institution**
  http://www.mnh.si.edu/nmnhweb.html

Physics

- **American Institute of Physics**
  http://www.aip.org
- **PhysLink**
  http://www.physlink.com/
- **Physics Resources, Case Western Reserve University**
  http://erebus.phys.cwru.edu/phys/resource/resources.html

Science

- **National Academy of Sciences**
  http://www4.nationalacademies.org/nas/nashome.nsf

Zoology

- **Smithsonian Zoology**
  http://www.si.edu/resource/faq/nmnh/zoology.htm

Business

- **All Business Network**
  http://www.all-biz.com/
- **American Institute of Certified Public Accountants**
  http://www.aicpa.org/
- **Commercenet**
  http://www.commerce.net/
- **Hoover's Online**
  http://www.hoovers.com/
- **Open Market**
  http://www.openmarket.com/

For more Web resources, see inside the front and back covers

Doing Research on the Web

CHAPTER 8

The Web as a Research Tool

Web vs. libraries

You may have heard people say that you can find any information you want on the Web. In reality, relatively few published books are available in their entirety on the Web. You may also have heard someone say that everything on the Web is advertising or garbage. Certainly a great deal of what's on the Web is advertising, and since no one is in charge of what appears on the Web, there is also a great deal of misinformation and highly biased information. But when you read something in print, it is not necessarily accurate and unbiased either. Books offer many examples of people witnessing the same event and later writing about it in ways so different that it's hard to believe they were in the same place at the same time. Likewise, there are many

127

examples of respected scientists examining the same data and reaching different conclusions. Walking through the doors of a library doesn't mean that everything you find there will be true, just as logging onto the Web doesn't mean everything is false.

A great deal of what you can find in a large library is not on the Web. Most books, films, recordings, scholarly journals, and older copies of newspapers are not available. Current journals and newspapers may be available on the Web only by subscription. But by the same token, the Web offers you some resources for current topics that would be difficult or impossible to find in libraries. The keys are knowing where you are most likely to find current and accurate information about the particular question you are researching and knowing how to access that information.

Applying your knowledge and experience

If you want something that can be located in an organization with a specific order, usually you can find it. The classic example is the telephone directory. If you know the name of the person you're looking for and the person is listed in the directory, you get the phone number fast. Likewise, if you know a newspaper article was published on a certain day and you have access to old copies on microfilm or on the Web, you can find it easily.

All too often, you can't rely on organizational systems as straightforward as the alphabet or dates for doing research on the Web. But when you think about it, a lot of the searching you do in daily life requires intelligent guesswork. The Web can feel like shopping in an unfamiliar grocery story, where it's difficult to find what you're looking for once you venture beyond the equivalents of the dairy and meat counters.

The Web is more like a world-wide bazaar filled with millions of people displaying their wares than a large grocery store, but like an unfamiliar grocery store, you often have to rely on multiple strategies and your past experience to find what you're looking for. There's an art to doing research on the Web. But like library research, you need to know what kinds of information you are looking for and have a plan for finding it. Likely you will have to modify this plan as you proceed.

What you can find on the Web

Take a concrete, real-life example. Sooner or later in life, most people suffer from lower back pain. In chronic cases, lower back pain can extend down one leg to the foot, a condition called *sciatica*. In many cases, sciatica is caused by a *herniated disc*—when a disc ruptures and allows part of the nucleus to be pushed into the spinal canal, where it presses on the spinal nerves causing pain. If you enter *sciatica* or *herniated disc* on a search engine, you will find an extraordinary number of Web sites that discuss each term—sites ranging from medical journals and medical school sites, the official sites of The American Association of Neurological Surgeons and The National Institutes of Health, advertising sites for chiropractors and physical therapists, and links to many discussion groups where people who have sought treatment discuss their experiences. While the Web is not a substitute for sound medical advice, you can get a sense of the diversity of current opinion from the Web. This diversity, however, can seem overwhelming. A good way to begin is to make a first pass to see how much is out there, then evaluate the kinds of information you find.

Planning Your Research

You do research every day. If you look up movie reviews to decide what you want to see or visit banks to find out where you can get the best deal on checking or go to the Web to find out what new music is available on MP3, you are doing research. If you become curious enough to look something up, you are doing research. Much of the time, however, these activities aren't thought of as research. In college, research means both investigating existing knowledge that is stored on computers and in libraries and creating new knowledge through original analysis, surveys, experiments, and theorizing. When you begin a research task, it's important to think about how to proceed.

1. **Analyze the research task.** If you have an assignment that requires research, it pays to look closely at what you are being asked to do. The assignment may ask you to review, compare, survey, analyze, evaluate, or prove something true or untrue. The purpose of your research will help guide your strategies for research.

2. **Find a subject that you are interested in.** Research can be enjoyable if the questions you ask are meaningful to you. The most exciting part of doing research lies in making small discoveries. You may need to do some browsing first to find to find a topic.

3. **Make sure that you can do a thorough job of research.** If you select a topic that is too broad, such as free speech and the Internet, you will not be able to do an adequate job. A question that might be researched in a limited paper or Web site is whether consumers have the right to record digital audio for their own use.

4. **Give yourself enough time.** You should expect to find a few dead ends, and you may need to start down another path. Even if you are fortunate enough to find a topic you can stay with, you should expect to focus your topic as you proceed.

Using Online Library Resources

The distinction between doing research online and in the library is becoming blurrier as more and more library resources are now online. Many colleges and universities have most of the major resources in their reference rooms online. Paper card catalogs are not being updated, so if you look for a book published in the last decade, you must use the online catalog. Newspapers, scholarly journals, and government documents are increasingly being archived in digital form. And all these resources are now being indexed online, so knowing how to search online catalogs is the fastest way to find where most information is located, even if it is in print. You are not limited to just your own library or even libraries in the United States. You can find links to online catalogs from libraries in over 90 countries on Libweb (http://sunsite.berkeley.edu/Libweb/).

Finding books

Nearly all libraries now shelve books according to the Library of Congress Classification System, which uses a combination of letters and numbers to give you the book's unique location in the library. The Library of Congress call number begins with a letter or letters that represent the broad subject area into which the book is classified. You can search the Library of Congress's online catalog (http://lcweb .loc.gov/catalog/) to help you find out how your subject might be indexed.

Suppose you want to do research on attention deficit disorder. Start with a "browse" search on the Library of Congress's online catalog (see Figure 8.1).

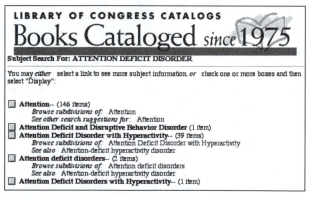

LIBRARY OF CONGRESS CATALOGS

Books Cataloged *since* 1975

Subject Search For: ATTENTION DEFICIT DISORDER

You may *either* select a link to see more subject information, *or* check one or more boxes and then select "Display":

- ☐ **Attention**-- (146 items)
    Browse subdivisions of: Attention
    See other search suggestions for: Attention
- ☐ **Attention Deficit and Disruptive Behavior Disorder** (1 item)
- ☐ **Attention Deficit Disorder with Hyperactivity**-- (39 items)
    Browse subdivisions of: Attention Deficit Disorder with Hyperactivity
    See also Attention-deficit hyperactivity disorder
- ☐ **Attention deficit disorders**-- (2 items)
    Browse subdivisions of: Attention deficit disorders
    See also Attention-deficit hyperactivity disorder
- ☐ **Attention Deficit Disorders with Hyperactivity**-- (1 item)

FIGURE 8.1   The Library of Congress's online catalog

The catalog will give you a choice of books cataloged before and after 1975, and of course you will want the newer books since attention deficit disorder is a relatively new concept. Next, select **Subject,** type "attention deficit disorder" in the box and click **Browse.**

The search gives you an extensive lists of topics. If you select the topic "Attention deficit-hyperactivity disorder (ADHD)," you get to a screen that notes 233 items and allows you to browse subdivisions of the topic.

```
☐ Attention-deficit disordered youth-- (5 items)
      Browse subdivisions of:  Attention-deficit disordered youth
☐ Attention-deficit hyperactivity disorder-- (1 item)
☐ Attention-deficit hyperactivity disorder-- (233 items)
      Browse subdivisions of:  Attention-deficit hyperactivity disorder
      See other search suggestions for:  Attention-deficit hyperactivity disorder
      See also   Attention deficit disorder with hyperactivity
      See also   Attention deficit disorders
      See also   Hyperactive child syndrome
      See also   Hyperkinetic syndrome
Attention-deficit hyperactivity disorder in adoles
      See   Attention-deficit disorder in adolescence
```

If you click on *"Browse subdivisons"* of ADHD, you get a list of subdivisions. These subdivisions can give you ideas for how to narrow your topic and keywords to use in searches.

```
☐ Attention-deficit hyperactivity disorder--Diagnosi (9 items)
      See other search suggestions for:  Attention-deficit hyperactivity disorder--Diagnosi
☐ Attention-deficit Hyperactivity disorder--Diet the (9 items)
☐ Attention-deficit hyperactivity disorder--Environm (1 item)
☐ Attention-deficit hyperactivity disorder--Epidemio (1 item)
☐ Attention-deficit hyperactivity disorder--Etiology (2 items)
☐ Attention-deficit hyperactivity disorder--Exercise (1 item)
☐ Attention-deficit hyperactivity disorder--Fiction (10 items)
☐ Attention-deficit Hyperactivity disorder--Genetic (2 items)
☐ Attention-deficit hyperactivity disorder--Handbook (5 items)
☐ Attention-deficit hyperactivity disorder--Homeopat (1 item)
☐ Attention-deficit hyperactivity disorder-- Juvenile (14 items)
```

Keyword searches

Subject searches use one or more search terms or keywords. To narrow your search, you can combine search terms with AND. For example, you may have read or heard that ADHD tends to run in families, so there are likely genetic influences. You can do additional searches using "attention deficit-hyperactivity disorder" AND "genetics" to narrow the topic. Most search tools also allow you to use OR to retrieve sites that include either term. Note that replacing AND with OR in the previous search would yield very different results, since using OR would make the search retrieve all sites about ADHD and all sites about genetics, not just sites related to genetic influences on ADHD.

Finding articles

Articles in scholarly journals, magazines, and newspapers are indexed much the same way. These indexes are located in the reference area of your library, and some or all may be available on your library's Web site. Some indexes contain the full text of articles. Others give you a citation, which you then have to find in your library. You can find the location of scholarly journals, magazines, and newspapers in your library's online catalog using the title search. General indexes include:

- **ArticleFirst.** Indexes over 13,500 journals in business, humanities, medicine, science, and social sciences.
- **Biography Index.** Indexes biographies, autobiographies, and interviews in 2,700 journals and 1,800 books.
- **CARL Uncover.** Citations to over 17,000 multidisciplinary journals.
- **Expanded Academic ASAP.** Index to 1600 periodicals, some with full text articles available.
- **LEXIS/NEXIS Academic Universe.** Full text of a wide range of newspapers, magazines, government and legal documents, and company profiles from around the world.
- **Periodical Abstracts.** Current events and business news from 600 periodicals.
- **Readers' Guide Abstracts.** Indexes popular periodicals.

In addition, there are many specialized indexes which list citations to journal articles in various fields.

Knowing which kind of articles you want to look for—scholarly, trade, or popular—will help you select the right index. Many indexes, however, include more than one type of journal. Although the difference between types of journals is not always obvious, you should be able to judge whether a journal is scholarly, trade, or popular by its characteristics.

Scholarly journals

Articles in scholarly journals are typically written by scholars in the field, usually affiliated with a university or research center. Articles are usually long, report original research, have few illustrations or advertisements, and include footnotes or a list of works cited at the end. They assume knowledge of the discipline and are written for others in the same field. Examples of scholarly journals include: *American Journal of Mathematics, College English, JAMA: Journal of the American Medical Association, Psychological Reports.*

Trade journals

Articles in trade journals are frequently related to practical job concerns. Articles usually do not report original research and have few or no footnotes or works cited at the end. Items of interest to people in particular professions and job listings are typical features, and advertisements are aimed at people in the specific field. Examples of trade journals include: *Advertising Age, Byte, PC Computing, Teacher Magazine.*

Popular journals

Articles in popular journals are short and often illustrated with color photographs. Articles are written by staff writers or freelancers and seldom have footnotes or acknowledge where their information came from. Advertisements are aimed at the general public, and copies can be bought at newsstands. Some popular journals: *Cosmopolitan, Time, Sports Illustrated, GQ.*

Follow these steps to find articles:

1. Select an index appropriate to your subject.
2. Search the index using relevant subject heading(s).
3. Print or copy the complete citation to the article(s).
4. Print or copy the full text if it is available.
5. If the full text is not available, check the periodicals holdings to see if your library has the journal.

Using Search Engines

Search engines designed for the Web work in ways similar to book and periodical indexes and your library's online catalog. Keep in mind two important differences. First, online catalogs and most indexes do not give you the full text but only a citation that you can use to find the printed item. Web search engines take you directly to the item, which, in most cases, does not exist except on the Web. Second, catalogs and online indexes do some screening in their selection of items. Search engines take you potentially to everything on the Web—hundreds of millions of pages in all. Consequently, you have to work harder to limit searches on the Web or else you can be deluged with tens of thousands of items.

Kinds of search engines

A search engine is a set of programs which sort through millions of items with incredible speed. There are three basic kinds of search engines:

1. **Keyword search engines** (e.g., AltaVista, Hotbot, Lycos, Northern Light). Keyword search engines use both a robot, which moves through the Web capturing information about Web sites, and an indexer, which organizes the

information found by the robot. They give different results because they assign different weights to the information they find. They often use words in the title of a Web site or words in a meta tag (see Chapter 10) to order the results they report.

2. **Web directories** (e.g., Britannica, Looksmart, Webcrawler, Yahoo). Web directories classify Web sites into categories and are the closest equivalent to the cataloging system used by libraries. On most directories professional editors decide how to index a particular Web site. Web directories also allow keyword searches.

3. **Metasearch agents** (e.g., Dogpile, Metafind, Metacrawler). Metasearch agents allow you to use several search engines simultaneously. While the concept is sound, metasearch agents are limited by the number of hits they can return and the inability to handle advanced searches.

Tips on search engines

If you don't have much experience with search engines, try out a few different ones until you find one or two favorites, and then learn how to use them well. Keyword search engines can be frustrating because they turn up so much, but you will become better with practice.

- To start your search, open your browser and select **Search.** You will be offered a selection of Web navigators and search engines.
- To use a keyword search, enter a word, name or phrase. Many search engines require you to use quotation marks to indicate a phrase or full name. If you type Gwyneth Paltrow without quotation marks, you will get hits for all instances of "Gwyneth" and all instances of "Paltrow."
- When you want the search to retrieve any form of a word, for example "ADHD" and both "child" and "children," you can use "child*" to get both terms. The * is sometimes referred to as a "wild card."

- Most search engines will only retrieve exact matches to the terms you use in your search request. Try all the variations you can think of if you want to do a thorough search.
- Some search engines use a plus sign (+) to indicate that a term is required (as in +ADHD +children) and a minus sign (-) to indicate that sites containing that term should not be included. For example, +ADHD -children will exclude sites on ADHD that mention children. Other search engines use AND, OR, and NOT in capital letters.
- Use the "search tips" or "help" on a search engine for particular advice.

The art of keyword searches

Keywords identify the subject's central concepts. Many are so obvious that even people completely new to a topic would recognize them intuitively. But even when they are obvious, sometimes they turn up way too much material. For example, an Excite search (on June 24, 1999) turned up 108,690 matches for a search on "attention deficit disorder." Clearly, this phrase is way too general to be an effective search term. Combining "ADHD" with "children" gets the number down to 4480, still way too many hits. Adding "genetics" (+ADHD +children +genetics) reduces the number of hits to 314—much better, but still unmanageable. If you are interested in treatments and add the drug Ritalin to the list (+ADHD +children +genetics +Ritalin), you get the number down to 61 (see Figure 8.2).

Excite offers the option of further refining your search by creating additional searches using the "Search for more documents like this one" command after each entry.

Searching by subject

If you have a topic in mind, a keyword search is usually the most efficient way to find sites on that topic. But when you are not certain of your topic or when you want to get a broad, general sense of what's

FIGURE 8.2 Excite search: +ADHD +children +genetics +Ritalin (http://search.excite.com)

available, you can browse the Web using the subject indexes offered by Web directories like Yahoo. To use the subject search, ignore the keyword search box and select one of the subject fields listed below it. You will get a list of narrower topics within the field, from which you can select still narrower subject areas. A subject search, however, is limited by what is already indexed in a Web directory. Expect different Web directories to produce different results and the searches to be less comprehensive than keyword searches.

To begin a subject search on ADHD using Yahoo, begin by selecting the appropriate major category (see Figure 8.3). For ADHD, "Health" is the obvious choice. Under "Diseases and Conditions" is a long list, on which you can find Attention Deficit Disorder. Before you examine individual Web sites, you can surmise that the use of Ritalin for treating ADHD is controversial (see Figure 8.4).

Evaluating Sources

All electronic search tools share a common problem: they often give you way too many sources. Web search engines not only pull up thousands of hits on many searches, but the quality varies a great deal too. No one regulates or checks information put on the Web, and it's no surprise that much of what is on the Web is highly opinionated or false information. Some Web sites are put up as jokes. A famous site created by a professor at Mankato State University in Minnesota describes Mankato as a tropical paradise, where, according to the site, the temperature in many neighborhoods never drops below 70 degrees in the winter because steam seeps up through the Earth's crust and heats the air (http://www.lme.mankato.msus.edu/mankato/mankato.html). It describes attractions including an underwater city, an ancient pyramid, and whalewatching in the Minnesota River. (Apparently enough people were gullible enough to drive to Mankato expecting to see these attractions because the site now has a prominent disclaimer.)

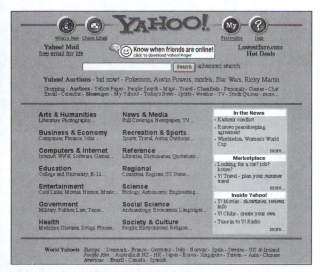

FIGURE 8.3 Yahoo (http://www.yahoo.com)

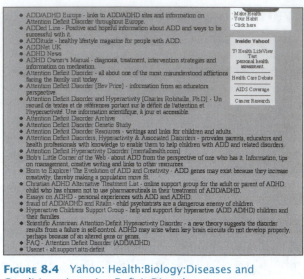

- ADD/ADHD Europe - links to ADD/ADHD sites and information on Attention Deficit Disorder throughout Europe.
- ADDed Line - Positive and hopeful information about ADD and ways to be successful with it.
- ADDitude - healthy lifestyle magazine for people with ADD.
- ADDNet UK
- ADHD News
- ADHD Owner's Manual - diagnosis, treatment, intervention strategies and information on medication.
- Attention Deficit Disorder - all about one of the most misunderstood afflictions facing the family unit today.
- Attention Deficit Disorder [Bev Price] - information from an educators perspective.
- Attention Deficit Disorder and Hyperactivity [Charles Robitaille, Ph.D] - Un recueil de textes et de références portant sur le déficit de l'attention et l'hyperactivité. Une information scientifique, à jour et accessible.
- Attention Deficit Disorder Archive
- Attention Deficit Disorder Genetic Study
- Attention Deficit Disorder Resources - writings and links for children and adults.
- Attention Deficit Disorders, Hyperactivity & Associated Disorders - provides parents, educators and health professionals with knowledge to enable them to help children with ADD and related disorders.
- Attention Deficit Hyperactivity Disorder [mentalhealth.com]
- Bob's Little Corner of the Web - about ADD from the perspective of one who has it. Information, tips on management, creative writing and links to other resources
- Born to Explore! The Evolution of ADD and Creativity - ADD genes may exist because they increase creativity, thereby making a population more fit.
- Christian ADHD Alternative Treatment List - online support group for the adult or parent of ADHD child who has chosen not to use pharmaceuticals in their treatment of ADD/ADHD.
- Essays on ADHD - personal experiences with ADD and ADHD
- fraud of ADD/ADHD and Ritalin - child psychiatrists are a dangerous enemy of children
- Hyperactive Childrens Support Group - help and support for hyperactive (ADD AD/HD) children and their families.
- Scientific American: Attention-Deficit Hyperactivity Disorder - a new theory suggests the disorder results from a failure in self-control. ADHD may arise when key brain circuits do not develop properly, perhaps because of an altered gene or genes.
- FAQ - Attention Deficit Disorder (ADD/ADHD)
- Usenet - alt.support.attn-deficit

FIGURE 8.4 Yahoo: Health:Biology:Diseases and Conditions:Attention Deficit Disorder (http://dir.yahoo.com/Health/Diseases_and_Conditions/Attention_Deficit_Disorder/)

Other misleading Web sites, however, are not put up for amusement. Many prominent Web sites draw imitators who want to cash in on the commercial visibility. The Web site for the Campaign for Tobacco-Free Kids (http://www.tobaccofreekids.org) has an imitator (http://www.smokefreekids.com) that sells software for anti-smoking education. The **.com** URL is often a tip-off that a site has a profit motive, but other sites are more misleading. The government of Tunisia put up a site on human rights in that country boasting of great progress with a URL that suggests the site belongs to Amnesty International (http://www.amnesty-tunisia.org). Nothing on the site specifically identifies it as the voice of the government (See Figure 8.5). Amnesty International put up a site (http://www.amnesty.org/tunisia/) that includes a point-by-point refutation of what it describes as "official Tunisian propaganda" (see Figure 8.6).

Approach Web sites with an eye toward evaluating content. The Web site of the National Institute of Mental Health on ADHD can be verified in several

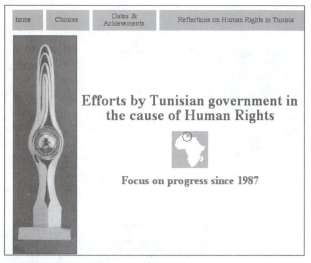

FIGURE 8.5 Government site on human rights in Tunisia (http://www.amnesty-tunisia.org/)

ways, beginning with the URL. If it is a government agency, it should have a **.gov** URL (see Figure 8.7).

Other sites may have equally reliable information, but be prepared to look closely. For example, the Web site "The Fraud of Child Psychiatry," lists MDs as authorities (see Figure 8.8). But a quick glance at the site reveals that it is designed to sell books that take strong positions against psychotherapeutic drugs such as Prozac, Xanax, and

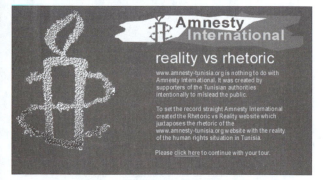

FIGURE 8.6 Amnesty International site on human rights in Tunisia (http://www.amnesty.org/tunisia/)

NIMH
National Institute
of Mental Health

Attention Deficit Hyperactivity Disorder

Understanding the Problem

What are the symptoms of ADHD?

Can any other conditions conditions produce these symptoms?

Can other disorders accompany ADHD?

What causes ADHD?

Getting Help

How is ADHD identified and diagnosed?

What are the educational options?

What treatments are available?

Sustaining Hope

Can ADHD be outgrown or cured?

What hope does research offer?

What are sources of information and support?

I Home I Mental Disorder Info I

Attention Deficit Hyperactivity Disorder

Imagine living in a fast-moving kaleidoscope, where sounds, images, and thoughts are constantly shifting. Feeling easily bored, yet helpless to keep your mind on tasks you need to complete. Distracted by unimportant sights and sounds, your mind drives you from one thought or activity to the next. Perhaps you are so wrapped up in a collage of thoughts and images that you don't notice when someone speaks to you.

For many people, this is what it's like to have Attention Deficit Hyperactivity Disorder, or ADHD. They may be unable to sit still, plan ahead, finish tasks, or be fully aware of what's going on around them. To their family, classmates or coworkers, they seem to exist in a whirlwind of disorganized or frenzied activity. Unexpectedly--on some days and in some situations--they seem

FIGURE 8.7 Attention Deficit Hyperactivity Disorder site, National Institute of Mental Health (http://www.nimh.nih.gov/publicat/adhd.htm)

The Fraud of Child Psychiatry, ADD/ADHD, Attention Deficit Disorder, and Ritalin.

"...This elementary fact makes the child psychiatrist one of the most dangerous enemies not only of children, but also of adults who care for the two precious and most vulnerable things in life - children and liberty. Child psychology and child psychiatry cannot be reformed. They must be abolished." - Thomas Szasz M.D., *Cruel Compassion.*

"The pediatrician's wanton prescription of powerful drugs indoctrinates children from birth with the philosophy of 'a pill for every ill.'"... "Doctors are directly responsible for hooking millions of people on prescription drugs. They are also indirectly responsible for the plight of millions more who turn to illegal drugs because they were taught at an early age that drugs can cure anything - including psychological and emotional conditions - that ails them. " - Robert S. Mendelsohn, M.D., *How to Raise a Healthy Child...In Spite of Your Doctor.*

Fred A. Baughman, M.D. - Immunize Your Child Against ADD   Peter R. Breggin, M.D. - Toxic Psychiatry

Peter R. Breggin, M.D. - Talking Back to Ritalin   Ann B. Tracy, PhD - Psychiatric Drugs

Fred A. Baughman, M.D. - What You Should Know About ADD   If You Need Help

A Dose of Sanity, by Sydney Walker III, M.D.

"A brilliant expose of the scandalous failure of modern psychiatry...If your doctor recommends Prozac, Xanax, Ritalin, or psychotherapy for your "mental" problems, read this book first. It just might save your life."
- Bernard Rimland, PhD., Director of the Autism Research Institute

If you are currently being treated for depression, anxiety or panic disorder, attention deficit disorder, a sleeping disorder, or any of a

FIGURE 8.8 "Fraud of child psychiatry" site (http://www.geocities.com/HotSprings/8568/)

Ritalin. The URL (http://www.geocities.com/Hot Springs/8568/) tells you that this site is on a "free" server, not an institutional site. It could have been put up by anyone.

Determining the reliability and relevance of sources is not a new problem with the Web. Print sources contain their share of biased, inaccurate, and misleading information. The major difference is that it is much more expensive to print and distribute a book. Web sites can be put up and changed quickly. Although print and Web sources differ in many ways, criteria developed for evaluating print sources can be applied to the Web.

Traditional criteria for evaluating print sources

Over the years librarians have developed a set of criteria for evaluating print sources.

1. **Source.** Who published the book or article? Scholarly books and articles in scholarly journals are reviewed by experts in the field before they are published. They are generally more reliable than popular magazines and books, which tend to emphasize what is sensational or entertaining at the expense of accuracy and comprehensiveness.
2. **Author.** Who wrote the book or article? What qualifications does the author possess?
3. **Timeliness.** How current is the source? If you are researching a fast developing subject such as treating ADHD, then currency is very important. Currency might not be so important for an older subject.
4. **Evidence.** Where does the evidence come from—facts, interviews, observations, surveys, or experiments? Is the evidence adequate to support the author's claims?
5. **Biases.** Can you detect particular biases of the author? How do the author's biases affect the interpretation offered?

6. **Advertising.** Is the advertising prominent in the journal or newspaper? How might the ads affect what gets printed?

Extending print criteria for evaluating Web sources

The criteria for evaluating print sources can be applied to Web sources if the special circumstances of the Web are acknowledged. For example, when you find a Web page using a search engine, often you go deep into a complex site without having any sense of the context for that page.

1. **Source.** Web sites sponsored by organizations often are as reliable as print sources. For example, major newspapers now make some or all of their reportage available on the Web. If a Web site doesn't indicate ownership, then you have to make judgments about who put it up and why.
2. **Author.** Often Web sites give no information about their authors other than an email address. In such cases it is difficult or impossible to determine the author's qualifications.
3. **Timeliness.** Many Web pages do not list when they were last updated, thus you cannot determine their currency. Furthermore, there are thousands of deserted "ghost" sites on the Web—sites that the owners have abandoned but still turn up in results on search engines.
4. **Evidence.** The accuracy of any evidence found on the Web is often hard to verify. The most reliable information on the Web stands up to the tests of print evaluation, with clear indication of the sponsoring organization.
5. **Biases.** Many Web sites announce their viewpoint on controversial issues but others conceal their attitude with a reasonable tone and seemingly factual evidence such as statistics.
6. **Advertising.** Many Web sites are "infomercials" aimed at getting you to buy a product or ser-

vice. While they might contain useful information, they are no more trustworthy than other forms of advertising.

Keeping Track of Your Research

Before the days of the Web and personal computers, most research projects involved taking notes on notecards. While cumbersome, this method has the advantage of allowing you spread out the notecards to get an overview of how the information you gathered might be connected. Today many people copy information to files and make notes in those. The advantage of this method is that you don't have to retype anything. Just as in constructing a Web site, you benefit greatly in the long run if you stay organized.

Get full bibliographic information when you make notes

For books, write down the author's name, title of the book, place of publication, publisher, and date of publication. This information is on the front and back of the title page. For journals, get the author's name, title of the article, title of the journal, issue of the journal, date of the issue, and page numbers. For Web sites, record the name of the page, the author if listed, the sponsoring organization if listed, the date the site was posted, the date you visited, and the complete URL.

Copy the sources you plan to use in your paper or Web site

Web sources and other electronic sources allow you to copy the text, which can eliminate errors caused by retyping. Likewise, photocopies ensure accuracy in copying print sources. In either case make sure you attach full bibliographic information to the file or photocopy. It's easy to get confused about where the source came from.

Using and Documenting Sources

CHAPTER 9

The Purpose of Documenting Sources

From a student's point of view, documenting sources can seem like learning Latin—something obscure and complicated that has little use in daily life. You don't see footnotes or lists of works cited in magazines and newspapers, so why are they such a big deal in college writing? Careful documenting of sources, however, is essential to develop knowledge, allowing scholars and researchers to build on the work of other scholars and researchers. The broad body of knowledge that allows a scholar to reinterpret the fall of the Roman Empire or a researcher to advance a new hypothesis about how moving plates shape the surface of Mars has accumulated over many years.

Knowledge building

Knowledge is built through ongoing conversations that take place in writing as well as talking. The practice of citing sources provides a disciplinary map, indicating the

147

conversation in which the writer is participating and how that writer responds to what has been said before. Often knowledge building does not move in a straight line but reflects wrong turns and backtracking. Tracing these movements would be extremely difficult if writers did not acknowledge their sources. Accurate referencing of sources gives readers the opportunity to consult those sources. For example, historians who write about the distant past must rely on different kinds of evidence including letters, records, public documents, newspaper articles, legal records, and other material from that time; plus, they take into account the work of contemporary scholars. Other historians working in the same area must be able to find and read these same primary sources to assess the accuracy of the interpretation. The system of citing sources requires that summaries and paraphrases be accurate, any strings of words taken from the original be set off in quotation marks, and full information be provided to locate the source.

Fairness

Another basic issue is fairness. If one historian draws on the interpretation of another historian, she should give the other historian credit. In this respect, citing sources builds community both with writers of the present and those of the past. When you begin to read the published research in an academic discipline, you become aware of that community. But the issue of fairness also is part of much larger sets of issues surrounding the concepts of intellectual property and scholastic honesty—issues that need to be carefully considered when you use sources.

Intellectual Property and Scholastic Honesty

Do certain songs instantly remind you of other songs? Many people think that the Offspring's hit song, "Why Don't You Get a Job?" sounds a lot like the Beatles' "Ob-La-Di, Ob-La-Da"—so much so that a Southern California DJ began mocking the resemblance by playing a composite version, splicing parts of the Beatles' song into the Offspring's hit. Likewise, when you saw a Furby doll for the first time, did it remind you of Gizmo from the Warner Bros. movies *Gremlins* and *Gremlins 2: The New Batch*? Warner Bros. executives certainly noted the similarity. These are but two recent examples of the complicated issues surrounding the concepts of intellectual property and copyright.

Intellectual property and copyright

These concepts have a long history dating back to royal patent grants accompanying the development of printing in the late 1400s, when kings sought to control the production of printed books. The modern concept of copyright took shape in the 1700s. In 1710, the Statute of Anne was passed in England, giving authors the rights to what they produced for a limited duration: by the end of the century other countries, including the United States, had passed laws to protect written intellectual property. With the development of new technologies in the 20th century, these rights have been extended to music, recordings, photographs, films, radio and television broadcasts, computer software, and many other kinds of likenesses. Determining when these rights apply, however, can be difficult. While "Why Don't You Get a Job?" sounds a lot like "Ob-La-Di, Ob-La-Da," proving copyright infringement is not easy because so much of popular music sounds similar.

Plagiarism

Plagiarism is usually associated with writing, but the examples of "Why Don't You Get a Job?" and the Furby doll show that different kinds of work can be lifted and passed off as one's own. Plagiarism means claiming credit for someone else's intellectual work no matter whether it's to make money or get a better grade. And it's not strictly a question of intent. In another famous case involving plagiarism of a song, former Beatle George Harrison was found guilty of copying the melody of Ronnie Mack's "He's So Fine" for Harrison's "My Sweet Lord," even though the borrowing may well have been unconscious. Others have gotten into trouble through carelessness by taking notes from published sources but not acknowledging those sources. A number of famous people have had their reputations tarnished by accusations of plagiarism, and several prominent journalists have lost their jobs and careers for ripping off the work of other writers.

The Internet likely has increased instances of plagiarism in college. Many new sources of information are available on the Internet, and some students view the Internet as a big free buffet where they can grab anything, paste it in a file, and submit it as their own work. These students often do not realize that their instructors can recognize quickly when their writing style changes and that it's also easy to trace stolen sources on the Internet. Most colleges and universities consider plagiarism a serious form of cheating that deserves severe penalties including failure of a course for first-time offenders and expulsion for those who are caught cheating more than once. Colleges have to take a strong stance against plagiarism. They attempt to make the playing field level for all students; if some get by without doing the required work, it affects every other student. Professional schools and employers look down on graduates of schools which have a reputation for tolerating scholastic dishonesty. And students who blatantly plagiarize often do not realize how much harm they might do to themselves down the road. Employers do not want to hire students who have been caught cheating.

Copyright, plagiarism, and the Web

The issues of intellectual property and copyright are far from settled concerning the Web. Copyright law is designed to protect the financial interests of the copyright holder; thus if you use a single image from a site and your motive is not for profit, then the copyright owner has to establish that your use of that image caused the owner financial harm (see Fair Use Test at http://www.utsystem.edu/ogc/ intellectualproperty/copypol2.htm). It's unlikely that you will be sued for grabbing an image from another site. Nonetheless, it is still plagiarism if you take someone else's work without acknowledgment. It's only fair to give other people credit for the work they have done. Unless a site is clearly labeled for public use, ask permission when you take something from another site, and always give credit to the source.

How to Avoid Plagiarism

You know that copying someone else's paper word for word or taking an article off the Internet and turning it in as yours is plagiarism. That's plain stealing, and people who take that risk should know that the punishment can be severe. But if plagiarism also means using the words, ideas, melodies or images of someone else without acknowledging them, then the concept is much broader and more difficult to define. If you think about it, you might wonder if it is possible to avoid plagiarizing in the strictest sense when you write. How many phrases and ideas are truly original? And how can you know where every idea comes from?

What you don't have to document

Fortunately, common sense rules with issues of academic plagiarism. The standards of documentation are not so strict that the source of every fact you cite must be acknowledged. Suppose you are writing about the causes of maritime disasters and you want to know how many people drowned when the *Titanic* sank on April 15, 1912. Your college makes available to students the *Encyclopaedia Britannica Online*, so you go to the *Britannica* Web site and find out the death toll was around 1,500. Since this fact is available in many reference works, you would not need to cite the *Britannica Online* as the source. But let's say you want to challenge the version of the sinking offered in the 1998 movie *Titanic*, which repeats the usual explanation that the *Titanic* side-swiped an iceberg, ripping a long gash along the hull that caused the ship to go down. In your reading, however, you discover that a September 1985 exploration of the wreck with an unmanned submersible did not find the long gash previously thought to have sunk the ship. The evidence from this exploration suggests that the force of the collision with the iceberg broke the seams in the hull, allowing water to flood *Titanic's* watertight compartments. You would need to cite the source of your information for the alternative version of the *Titanic's* demise.

What you do have to document

For any facts that are not easily found in general reference works, any statements of opinion, and any arguable claims, you should provide the source. Also you should cite the sources of any statistics, research findings, examples, graphs, charts, and illustrations. As a reader you should be skeptical about statistics and research findings if the source is not mentioned. When a writer does not cite the sources of statistics and research findings, there is no way of knowing how reliable they are or if the writer is making them up. From the writer's perspective, careful citing of sources gives you credibility. If you take your statistics from a source generally trusted, then your readers are more likely to trust your conclusions. When in doubt, always document the source.

Using words and ideas from a source

Most people who get into plagiarism trouble lift words from a source and use them without quotation marks. Where the line is drawn is easiest to illustrate with an example. In the passage below, Steven Johnson takes sharp issue with the metaphor of surfing applied to the Web:

> The concept of "surfing" does a terrible injustice to what it means to navigate around the Web. . . . What makes the idea of cybersurf so infuriating is the implicit connection drawn to television. Web surfing, after all, is a derivation of channel surfing—the term thrust upon the world by the rise of remote controls and cable panoply in the mid-eighties. . . . Applied to the boob tube, of course, the term was not altogether inappropriate. Surfing at least implied that channel-hopping was more dynamic, more involved, than the old routine of passive consumption. Just as a real-world surfer's enjoyment depended on the waves delivered up by the ocean, the channel surfer was at the mercy of the programmers and network executives. The analogy took off because it worked well in the one-to-many system of cable TV, where your navigational options were limited to the available channels.
>
> But when the term crossed over to the bustling new world of the Web, it lost a great deal of precision. . . . Web surfing and channel surfing are genuinely different pursuits; to imagine them as equivalents is to ignore the defining characteristics of each medium. Or at least that's what happens in theory. In practice, the Web takes on the greater burden. The television imagery casts the online surfer in the random, anesthetic shadow of TV programming, roaming from site to site like a CD player set on shuffle play. But what makes the online world so revolutionary is that the fact that there are connections between each stop on a Web itinerant's journey. The links that join those various destinations are links of association, not randomness. A channel surfer hops back and forth between different channels because she's bored. A Web surfer clicks on a link because she's interested.

> Johnson, Steven. *Interface Culture: How New Technology Transforms the Way We Create and Communicate*. New York: HarperCollins, 1997. 107–09.

If you were writing a paper or putting up a Web site that concerns Web surfing, you might want to mention the distinction that Johnson makes between channel surfing and surfing on the Web. Your options are to paraphrase the source or to quote it directly.

Quoting directly

If you quote directly, you must place quotation marks around all words you take from the original:

> One observer makes this contrast: "A channel surfer hops back and forth between different channels because she's bored. A Web surfer clicks on a link because she's interested" (Johnson 109).

Notice that the quote is introduced and not just dropped in. This example follows Modern Language Association (MLA) style, where the citation goes outside the quotation marks but before the period. References are made according to the author's last name, which refers you to the full citation in the works-cited list at the end. Following the author's name is the page number where the quote can be located. Notice also that there is no comma after the name. If you want to cite a newspaper article without a byline or another anonymous source, you use the first important word or two of the title to make the reference. The logic of this system is to enable you to find the reference easily in the list of works-cited.

If the author's name appears in the sentence, cite only the page number:

> According to Steven Johnson, "A channel surfer hops back and forth between different channels because she's bored. A Web surfer clicks on a link because she's interested" (109).

Paraphrasing

When you paraphrase, you put the idea of the source into your own words. You still need to include the reference for where the idea came from. The examples below illustrate what is and is not an acceptable paraphrase:

> **[Plagiarized]** Steven Johnson argues that the concept of "surfing" does a terrible injustice to what it means to navigate around the Web. What makes the idea of Web surfing infuriating is the association with television. Surfing is not a bad metaphor for channel hopping but it doesn't fit what people do on the Web. Web surfing and channel surfing are truly different activities; to imagine them as the same is to ignore their defining characteristics. A channel surfer skips around because she's bored while a Web surfer clicks on a link because she's interested (107–09).

Even though the source is listed, this paraphrase is unacceptable. Too many of the words in the original are used directly here, including much or all of entire sentences. When a string of words is lifted from a source and inserted without using quotation marks, the passage is plagiarized. Changing a few words in a sentence is not a paraphrase. Compare these two sentences:

> **[Source]** Web surfing and channel surfing are genuinely different pursuits; to imagine them as equivalents is to ignore the defining characteristics of each medium.

> **[Unacceptable paraphrase]** Web surfing and channel surfing are truly different activities; to imagine them as the same is to ignore their defining characteristics.

The paraphrase takes the structure of the original sentence and substitutes a few words. It is much too similar to the original.

A true paraphrase represents an entire rewriting of the idea from the source.

[Acceptable paraphrase] Stephen Johnson argues that "surfing" is a misleading term for describing how people navigate on the Web. He allows that "surfing" is appropriate for clicking across television channels because like ocean surfing, the viewer has to interact with what the networks and cable companies provide, just as the surfer has to interact with what the ocean provides. Web surfing, according to Johnson, operates at much greater depth and with much more consciousness of purpose. Web surfers actively follow links to make connections (107–09).

Even though there are a few words from the original in this paraphrase such as "navigate" and "connections," these sentences are original in structure and wording while accurately conveying the meaning of the source.

Incorporating Quotations Effectively

The purpose of using sources is to *support* what you have to say, not to say it for you. Next to plagiarism, the worst mistake you can make with sources is to string together a series of long quotations even if they are properly cited. This strategy leaves your readers wondering if you have anything to say. Relying too much on quotations from others also makes for a bumpy read.

When to use direct quotations and when to paraphrase

The rule of thumb in deciding when to include direct quotations and when to paraphrase lies in the importance of the original wording. If you want to refer to an idea or fact and the original wording is not critical, make the point in your own words. Save direct quotations for language that is memorable or gives the character of the source.

Suppose you are writing about the effects of the Internet on literacy, and you want to acknowledge those who maintain that the effects are largely negative. You find books by Sven Birkerts *(The Gutenberg Elegies: The Fate of Reading in an Electronic Age)*, Mark Slouka *(War of the Worlds: Cyberspace and the High-Tech Assault on Reality)*, and Clifford Stoll *(Silicon Snake Oil)* that argue that the Internet is a disorganized wasteland that discourages people from thinking for themselves. You also find a book by Jay David Bolter *(The Writing Space: The Computer, Hypertext and the History of Writing)*, someone more sympathetic to digital technologies who also sees them as a threat to the power of prose. You could paraphrase each argument but you realize that there are common fears that run through these books, so you decide to summarize these sources by making a list of the fears expressed. You want to use a direct quote from Bolter that articulates the cause of these fears. You might write:

> The rapid spread of the Internet has produced many critics such as Sven Birkerts, Mark Slouka, and Clifford Stoll, who all complain about how the Internet is destroying the foundations of literacy— that critical thinking and reflection, a sense of order, logical relations in texts, depth of analysis, trails of sources, and the reform mission of public discourse are going to be lost. Even those who take a more balanced view fear that the multimedia capability of the Web will undermine the power of prose. Jay David Bolter writes, "The new media . . . threaten to drain contemporary prose of its rhetorical possibilities. Popular prose responds with a desire to emulate computer graphics. Academic and other specialized forms respond by a retreat into jargon or willful anachronism" (270). The coming of the Web, however, does not have to be viewed as a loss to literacy. Images and words have long coexisted on the printed page and in manuscripts, but relatively few people possessed the resources to exploit the rhetorical potential of images combined with words.

You would include all four books in your works-cited list.

Block quotes

If a direct quote runs more than four lines, then it should be indented 10 spaces in MLA style or 5 spaces in APA style and double-spaced. When you indent a long quote this way, it is called a **block quote.** (There is an HTML <BLOCKQUOTE> tag that allows you to make block quotes on a Web page.) You still need to integrate block quotes into the text of your paper. Block quotations should be introduced by mentioning where the source came from. Note three points about form in the block quotation:

1. There are no quotation marks around the block quotation.
2. Words quoted in the original retain the double quotation marks.
3. The page number appears after the period at the end of the block quotation.

It's a good idea to include at least a sentence or two following the quote to describe its significance.

Whether long or short, you should double check that all quotations you use are accurate and that all words belonging to the original are either set off with quotation marks or placed in block quotes. You should also check to see if all sources are well integrated into the fabric of your paper.

MLA Documentation

Documentation standards vary by discipline, but the two styles used most frequently are the APA (American Psychological Association) style and the MLA (Modern Language Association) style. The APA style is followed in the social sciences and education, while the MLA style is the norm for humanities and fine arts disciplines. Both MLA and APA styles use parenthetical citations in the body and a works-cited list placed at the end.

The great advantage of a parenthetical citation system is that it eliminates the need for footnotes. Thus when the reader finds a reference to a source in the body, such as:

> One observer makes this contrast: "A channel surfer hops back and forth between different channels because she's bored. A Web surfer clicks on a link because she's interested" (Johnson 109).

she then can turn to the works-cited list and find the full citation:

> Johnson, Steven. <u>Interface Culture: How New Technology Transforms the Way We Create and Communicate</u>. New York: HarperCollins, 1997.

She can use the information in the citation to locate the book and check if the writer accurately represents Johnson and how the point quoted fits into Johnson's larger argument.

In the past, titles of books and periodicals were always underlined in the works-cited list even though they appear as italics when they are printed. This practice reflects the heritage of typewriters, where you could not switch over to italics. When writers underlined a word, the printer knew to set that word in italics. But when the Web became popular, underlining a word often signalled it was a link. (You can still set your browser to underline links or turn off the underlining.) For that reason it is better to use italics for titles of books and periodicals to avoid confusion when you put a works-cited list on a Web site. Underlining of titles is still preferred by the authors of MLA and APA style, who remain oriented to paper.

To create a works-cited list in MLA style, using the paper format convention of underlining titles, you should follow this format:

1. Center "Works Cited."
2. Double-space all entries. Indent all but first line five spaces.
3. Alphabetize entries by last name of authors or by title if no author is listed.
4. Underline the titles of books and periodicals (see Figure 9.1).

If you compile your works-cited list the old way by listing sources on notecards, then all you have to do when you finish your research is alphabetize the cards and type your works-cited list. For works with no author listed, alphabetize by the first content word in the title (ignore "a," "an," and "the"). If you do all your work on a computer, then make a works-cited file when you start your research and add each item you consult as you do your research. Either way, make sure to get all the information necessary for complete citations because it's difficult and sometimes impossible to recover later.

The more common citation formats in MLA style are listed below. If you have questions that these examples do not address, consult the *MLA Handbook for Writers of Research Papers* (fifth edition, 1999) and the *MLA Style Manual and Guide to Scholarly Publishing* (second edition, 1998).

Books

The basic format for books in the works-cited list includes:

1. Author's name (last name first).
2. Title (underlined or in italics).
3. Place of publication.
4. Short name of publisher.
5. Date of publication.

You find the exact title on the title page (not on the cover), the publisher, and the city (use the first city if several are listed). The date of publication is included in the copyright notice on the back of the title page.

Works Cited

Agre, Phil. "The Internet and Public Discourse." <u>First Monday</u> 3.3 (March 1998). 14 July 1999 <http://www.firstmonday.dk/issues/issue3_3/agre/>.

Kleiner, Kurt. "Calling All Geeks." <u>New Scientist</u> 15 May 1999: 10.

Mallia, Joseph. "Authorities React to Abuse of Tax-funded Internet." <u>Boston Herald</u> 13 May 1999: 6.

McCullough, Malcolm. <u>Abstracting Craft: The Practiced Digital Hand</u>. Cambridge, MA: MIT P, 1998.

Mendels, Pamela. "Non-Traditional Teachers More Likely to Use the Net." <u>New York Times on the Web</u> 26 May 1999. 19 June 1999 <http://www.nytimes.com/library/tech/99/05/cyber/education/26education.html>.

National Center for Education Statistics. "Internet Access in Public Education." February 1998. NCES. 4 Jan. 1999 <http://nces.ed.gov/pubs98/98021.html>.

"The Net Is Where the Kids Are." <u>Business Week</u> 10 May 1999: 44.

Wolfe, Joanna L. "Why Do Women Feel Ignored? Gender Differences in Computer-Mediated Classroom Interactions." <u>Computers and Composition</u> 16.1 (1999): 153-66.

FIGURE 9.1   MLA list of works cited

Book by one author
Johnson, Steven. <u>Interface Culture: How New Technology Transforms the Way We Create and Communicate</u>. New York: HarperCollins, 1997.

Book by two or more authors
McClelland, Deke, and Katrin Eismann. <u>Web Design Studio Secrets</u>. Foster City, CA: IDG Books, 1998.

Two or more books by the same author
Siegel, David. <u>Creating Killer Web Sites: The Art of Third-Generation Design</u>. Indianapolis, IN: Hayden, 1996.
———. <u>Secrets of Successful Web Sites: Project Management on the World Wide Web</u>. Indianapolis, IN: Hayden, 1997.

Translation
Martin, Henri-Jean. <u>The History and Power of Writing</u>. Trans. Lydia G. Cochrane. Chicago: U of Chicago P, 1994.

Edited book
Selzer, Jack, and Sharon Crowley, eds. <u>Rhetorical Bodies: Toward a Material Rhetoric</u>. Madison, WI: U of Wisconsin P, 1999.

One volume of a multivolume work
Habermas, Jürgen. <u>Lifeworld and System, A Critique of Functionalist Reason</u>. Trans. Thomas McCarthy. Boston: Beacon, 1987. Vol. 2 of <u>The Theory of Communicative Action</u>. 2 vols. 1984-1987.

Selection in an anthology or chapter in an edited collection
Baron, Dennis. "From Pencils to Pixels: The Stages of Literacy Technologies." <u>Passions, Pedagogies, and 21st Century</u>

Technologies. Ed. Gail E. Hawisher and
Cynthia L. Selfe. Logan: Utah State UP,
1999. 15-33.

Government document
Malveaux, Julianne. "Changes in the Labor
Market Status of Black Women." A Report
of the Study Group on Affirmative Action
to the Committee on Education and Labor.
U. S. 100th Cong., 1st sess. H. Rept. 100-
L. Washington: GPO, 1987. 213-55.

Bible
Holy Bible. King James Version.

[Note that the Bible is not underlined. No other publication information besides the version is necessary.]

Periodicals

The necessary items to include are:

1. Author's name (last name first).
2. Title of the article (inside quotation marks).
3. Title of the journal or magazine (underlined or
   in italics).
4. Volume number (for scholarly journals).
5. Date.
6. Page numbers.

Many scholarly journals are printed to be bound as
one volume, usually by year, with continuous pagination for that year. If, say, a scholarly journal is printed
in 4 issues and the first issue ends on page 226, then
the second issue will begin with page 227. For journals
that are continuously paginated, you do not need to
include the issue number. Some scholarly journals,
however, are paginated like magazines with each
issue beginning with page 1. For journals paginated by
issue, list the issue number along with the volume
(e.g., for the first issue of volume 9, you would put 9.1
in the entry after the title of the journal).

Article in a scholarly journal—continuous pagination

George, Diana, and John Trimbur. "The 'Communication Battle,' or Whatever Happened to the 4th C?" <u>College Composition and Communication</u> 50 (1999): 682-98.

Article in a scholarly journal—pagination by issue

Davis, Jim. "Rethinking Globalisation." <u>Race and Class</u> 40.2/3 (1999): 37-48.

Review

Berger, Sidney E. Rev. of <u>The Evolution of the Book</u>, by Frederick G. Kilgour. <u>Library Quarterly</u> 69 (1999): 402.

Magazine article

Barlow, John Perry. "Africa Rising: Everything You Know about Africa Is Wrong." <u>Wired</u> Jan. 1998: 142-58.

Newspaper article

WuDunn, Sheryl. "Japan Bets on a Wired World to Win Back Its Global Niche." <u>New York Times</u> 30 Aug. 1999, late ed.: A1+.

Letter to the editor

Cicerone, Ralph J. Letter. <u>Chronicle of Higher Education</u> 13 Sept. 1999: B12.

Editorial

"Phone Rage." Editorial. <u>Los Angeles Times</u> 31 Aug. 1999, final ed.: B6.

Online sources

Online sources pose special difficulties for systems of citing sources because they often change frequently and lack basic information. The format for citing a generic Web site includes:

1. Author's name (last name first).
2. Title of document in quotation marks.
3. Title of complete work or name of journal (underlined).
4. Date of Web publication or last update.
5. Sponsoring organization.
6. Date you visited.
7. URL <enclosed in angle brackets>.

This convention works fine for a works-cited list on paper. Putting anything in angle brackets on a Web site, however, will be interpreted as an HTML tag, and it will not show up on your Web page. To get the angle brackets on a Web page requires using a special name for the characters that begins with an ampersand (&) and ends with a semicolon (;). The special names for the angle brackets are:

< for   <
> for   >

You may have to go into the HTML file and type in these special names for the angle brackets if your Web page editor does not do it for you. You'll know that the conversion of the special names hasn't been made if the angle brackets and what's inside them do not show up on your Web page. The authors of the MLA style apparently were unaware of how HTML works when they decided on angle brackets.

Web site
Kaplan, Nancy. "E-literacies: Politexts, Hypertexts and Other Cultural Formations in the Late Age of Print." Rev. 17 Dec. 1997. 2 July 1999 <http://raven.ubalt .edu/staff/kaplan/lit/>.

Book on the Web
Rheingold, Howard. Tools for Thought: The People and Ideas of the Next Computer Revolution. New York, 1985. 1996.

Brainstorms. 4 Jan. 1999 <http://www
.well.com/user/hlr/texts/tftindex.html>.

Article in a scholarly journal on the Web
Agre, Phil. "The Internet and Public
Discourse." <u>First Monday</u> 3:3 (March
1998). 14 July 1999 <http://www.first
monday.dk/ issues/issue3_3/agre/>.

Article in a newspaper on the Web
Mendels, Pamela. "Non-Traditional Teachers
More Likely to Use the Net." <u>New York
Times on the Web</u> 26 May 1999. 19 June
1999 <http://www.nytimes.com/
library/tech/99/05/cyber/education/
26education.html>.

CD-ROM
Boyer, Paul, et al. <u>The Enduring Vision,
Interactive Edition</u>. 1993 ed. CD-ROM.
Lexington, MA: Heath, 1993.

Other sources

Television programs and films in most cases have
the title first followed by information about the
director, actors, and others depending on the needs
of readers.

Interview
McConaughey, Matthew. Telephone interview. 27 May 1999.

Unpublished dissertation
Friend, Christy. "Public Voices, Private Lives:
Promoting Responsible Public Discourse in
the Postmodern Writing Classroom." Diss.
U of Texas at Austin. 1997.

Film
<u>The Blair Witch Project</u>. Dir. Daniel Myrick,
Eduardo Sánchez. Perf. Heather Donahue,
Michael C. Williams, Joshua Leonard.
Haxan Films. 1999.

Television program
"The Attitude." Dir. Allan Arkush, Daniel Attias, et al. Writ. David E. Kelley. Perf. Calista Flockhart, Courtney Thorne-Smith. Ally McBeal 3 Nov. 1997.

Sound recording
Teceschi, Susan. Just Won't Burn. Tone-Cool Records, 1998.

Speech (no printed text)
Jobs, Steve. Remarks at Macworld. New York. 21 July 1999.

Speech (printed text)
Hawisher, Gail E. "Local Literacies on the World Wide Web: International Perspectives." Conf. on Coll. Composition and Communication. Atlanta. 25 March 1999.

APA Documentation

Social sciences disciplines including government, linguistics, psychology, sociology, and those in education most frequently use the APA (American Psychological Association) documentation style. The APA style has many similarities to the MLA style. Both styles use parenthetical references in the body of the text with complete bibliographical citations in the works-cited list at the end. For a detailed treatment, consult the *Publication Manual of the American Psychological Association, 4th edition* (1994).

The biggest difference is the emphasis on the date of publication in the APA style. When you cite an author's name in the body of your paper using APA style, you always include the date of publication. For example:

Johnson (1997) makes this contrast: "A channel surfer hops back and forth between different channels because she's bored. A Web surfer clicks on a link because she's interested" (p. 109).

Notice too that unlike the MLA style, the APA style includes the abbreviation for page (p.) in front of the page number. If the author's name is not mentioned in the sentence, the reference looks like this:

> One observer makes this contrast: "A channel surfer hops back and forth between different channels because she's bored. A Web surfer clicks on a link because she's interested" (Johnson, 1997, p. 109).

And unlike MLA, a comma is placed after the author's name.

The APA list of works cited is titled "References" (see Figure 9.2). Observe these guidelines when centering an APA-style reference list:

1. Center "References"
2. Double-space all entries. Indent all but first line five spaces.
3. Alphabetize entries by last name of authors or by title if no author is listed.
4. Notice that author's initials are listed rather than first names.
5. Notice that only the first words and proper nouns are capitalized in titles.
6. Underline or italicize the titles of books and periodicals; no quote marks for articles.
7. APA specifies a different format for work submitted for publication, so be sure to consult the *Publication Manual of the American Psychological Association* for the proper format.

The references list eliminates the need for footnotes. For works with no author listed, alphabetize by the first significant word in the title (ignore "a," "an," and "the").

References

Agre, P. (1998). The Internet and public discourse." <u>First Monday, 3</u>(3). Retrieved July 14,
1999 from the World Wide Web: http://
www.firstmonday.dk/issues/issue3_3/agre/

Kleiner, K. (1999, May 15). Calling all geeks.
<u>New Scientist,</u> 10.

Mallia, J. (1999, May 13). Authorities react to
abuse of tax-funded Internet. <u>Boston Herald,</u> 6.

McCullough, M. (1998). <u>Abstracting craft: The
practiced digital hand.</u> Cambridge, MA: MIT
Press.

Mendels, P. (1999, May 26). Nontraditional
teachers more likely to use the net. <u>New
York Times on the Web.</u> Retrieved June 19,
1999 from the World Wide Web:
http://www.nytimes.com/library/tech/99/0
5/cyber/education/ 26education.html

National Center for Education Statistics. (1998,
Feb.). Internet access in public education.
Retrieved May 21, 1998 from the World
Wide Web: http://nces.ed.gov/pubs98/
98021.html

The net is where the kids are. (1999, May 10).
<u>Business Week,</u> 44.

Wolfe, J. L. (1999). Why do women feel ignored?
Gender differences in computer-mediated
classroom interactions. <u>Computers and
Composition, 16</u>(1), 153-66.

FIGURE 9.2   APA reference list

Books

The basic format for listing books in the references list includes:

1. Author's name (last name first, initials).
2. Date of publication (in parentheses).
3. Title (underlined or in italics).
4. Place of publication.
5. Short name of publisher.

Use the abbreviation for pages (pp.) for chapters in a book.

Book by one author
Johnson, S. (1997). <u>Interface culture: How new technology transforms the way we create and communicate.</u> New York: HarperCollins.

Book by two or more authors
McClelland, D., & Eismann, K. (1998). <u>Web design studio secrets.</u> Foster City, CA: IDG Books.

Translation
Martin, H.-J. (1994). <u>The history and power of writing</u> (L. G. Cochrane, Trans.). Chicago: University of Chicago Press.

Edited book
Selzer, J., & Crowley, S. (Eds.). (1999). <u>Rhetorical bodies: Toward a material rhetoric.</u> Madison, WI: University of Wisconsin Press.

One volume of a multivolume work
de Selincourt, E., & Darbishire, H. (Eds.). (1958). <u>The poetical works of William Wordsworth</u> (Vol. 5). Oxford: Oxford University Press.

Selection in an anthology or chapter in an edited collection

Baron, D. (1999). From pencils to pixels: The stages of literacy technologies. In G. E. Hawisher & C. L. Selfe (Eds.), <u>Passions, pedagogies, and 21st century technologies.</u> (pp. 15-33). Logan: Utah State University Press.

Unpublished dissertation

Friend, C. (1997). Public voices, private lives: Promoting responsible public discourse in the postmodern writing classroom. Unpublished doctoral dissertation, University of Texas at Austin.

Periodicals

The necessary items to include are:

1. Author's name (last name first, initials).
2. Title of the article.
3. Title of the journal or magazine (underlined or in italics).
4. Volume number (for scholarly journals).
5. Date.
6. Page numbers.

For articles in newspapers, use the abbreviation for pages (p. or pp.).

Article in a scholarly journal—continuous pagination

George, D., & Trimbur, J. (1999). The "communication battle," or whatever happened to the 4th C? <u>College Composition and Communication, 50,</u> 682-98.

Article in a scholarly journal—pagination by issue

Davis, J. (1999). Rethinking globalisation. <u>Race and Class, 40</u>(2/3), 37-48.

Review
> Berger, S. E. (1999). [Review of the book <u>The evolution of the book</u>]. <u>Library Quarterly, 69,</u> 402.

Magazine article
> Barlow, J. P. (1998, January). Africa rising: Everything you know about Africa is wrong. <u>Wired,</u> 142-58.

Magazine article—no author listed
> The net is where the kids are. (1999, May 10). <u>Business Week,</u> 44.

Newspaper article
> Mallia, J. (1999, May 13). Authorities react to abuse of tax-funded Internet. <u>Boston Herald,</u> p. 6.

Electronic sources

The Web has become an important scholarly resource since the latest edition of the *Publication Manual of the American Psychological Association* appeared in 1994. APA likely will revise its guidelines in the next edition and has put up a Web site with a few examples (http://www.apa.org/journals/webref.html).

Web site
> Kaplan, N. (1997). E-literacies: Politexts, hypertexts and other cultural formations in the late age of print. (Rev. December 17, 1997). Retrieved July 2, 1999 from the World Wide Web: http://raven.ubalt.edu/staff/kaplan/lit/

Article in a scholarly journal on the Web
> Agre, P. (1998). The Internet and public discourse. <u>First Monday, 3</u> (3). Retrieved May 10, 1999 from the World Wide Web:

http://www.firstmonday.dk/issues/
issue3_3/agre/

Article in a newspaper on the Web

Mendels, P. (1999, May 26). Nontraditional teachers more likely to use the net. <u>New York Times on the Web.</u> Retrieved June 19, 1999 from the World Wide Web: http://www.nytimes.com/library/tech/99/05/cyber/education/26education.html

Film

Spielberg, S. (Director). (1998). <u>Saving Private Ryan</u> [Film]. Hollywood, CA: DreamWorks and Paramount.

Sound recording

Teceschi, S. (1998). <u>Just won't burn</u> [CD]. Newton, MA: Tone-Cool Records.

COS Documentation for Online Sources

In addition to the Web, the Internet introduces other kinds of electronic sources including USENET discussion groups, listservs, chat rooms, graphics files, online data bases, and email. Systems of referencing developed for print sources are not equipped for these new kinds of sources. Electronic sources usually do not have page numbers, and in many cases it is hard to identify the date of publication, the place, and even the author. There have been several efforts to extend existing documentation styles to accommodate these new genres. The most thorough effort to date is the 1998 *The Columbia Guide to Online Style* by Janice R. Walker and Todd Taylor.

Columbia Online Style (COS) is not an alternative to other established documentation styles, including MLA and APA, but instead offers guidelines about how the principles of those styles might be extended to new forms. It also uses parenthetical references within the text with the author and page number for MLA-type references and the author, date, and page number for APA-type references. Of course page numbers are often not present in electronic sources and cannot be referenced. Furthermore, some Web sites lack both author and title. For such sites, COS recommends using the file name (e.g., animation.html) for the reference in the text. Similarly, the date of posting is often missing. For APA-type references, COS recommends including the date of access for the publication date in day-month-year format (24 June 1999).

The basic formats recommended by COS follow those of MLA. For MLA-type references, include the following if available:

1. Author's last name, first name.
2. "Title of Document." Place within quotation marks.
3. *Title of Complete Work* [if applicable]. Use italics.
4. Version number [if applicable].
5. Date of document or last revision [if different from access date].
6. URL or access path.
7. Date of access in parentheses.

For APA-type references, include the following if available:

1. Author's last name, initials.
2. Date of document or last revision [if different from access date] in parentheses.
3. Title of document. Capitalize only the first word and any proper nouns.
4. *Title of complete work* [if applicable]. Use italics and capitalize only the first word and any proper nouns.
5. Version number [if applicable] in parentheses.
6. URL or access path.
7. Date of access in parentheses.

You can find many examples in addition to the ones listed below in *The Columbia Guide to Online Style* and on the COS Web site (http://www .columbia.edu/cu/cup/cgos/idx_basic.html).

Web site
(MLA)
Burke, Jesse. "A guide to interactive/self-help diagnosis sites on the Internet." 1 July 1999. http://www.tlc.utexas.edu/ courses/tlc321/final/JessieB'sProject/ Welcome.htm (3 Sept. 1999).

(APA)
Burke, J. (1999, July 1). A guide to interactive/self-help diagnosis sites on the Internet. http://www.tlc.utexas.edu/ courses/tlc321/final/JessieB'sProject/ Welcome.htm (3 Sept. 1999).

Web site, revised
Replace the publication date with the date of revision.
(MLA)
Kaplan, Nancy. "E-literacies: Politexts, Hypertexts and Other Cultural Formations in the Late Age of Print." Rev. 17 Dec. 1997. http://raven.ubalt.edu/staff/kaplan/ lit/ (2 July 1999).

(APA)
Kaplan, N. (1997). E-literacies: Politexts, hypertexts and other cultural formations in the late age of print. (Rev. 17 Dec. 1997). http://raven.ubalt.edu/staff/kaplan/lit/ (2 July 1999).

Web site of an organization, group, or corporation
Use the name of the organization, group, or corporation as the author. If the site is frequently updated, no publication date is given because it is the same as the date of access.
(MLA)
People for the Ethical Treatment of Animals. "Toxic Testing." http://www.peta-online .org/299/index.html (31 Aug. 1999).

(APA)
People for the Ethical Treatment of Animals. Toxic testing. http://www.peta-online .org/299/index.html (31 Aug. 1999).

Article in an online scholarly journal
(MLA)
Agre, Phil. "The Internet and Public Discourse." *First Monday* 3:3 (March 1998). http://www.firstmonday.dk/issues/ issue3_3/agre/ (10 May 1999).
(APA)
Agre, P. (1998). The Internet and public discourse. *First Monday, 3* (3). http://www .firstmonday.dk/issues/issue3_3/agre/ (10 May 1999).

Article from an online news service
(MLA)
Rao, Modanmohan. WorldTel in $100 M Community Initiative for Indian State. *Asia InternetNews* 10 Feb. 1999. http://asia .internet.com/1999/2/1003-india.html (16 June 1999).
(APA)
Rao, M. (1999, February 10). WorldTel in $100 M community initiative for Indian state. *Asia InternetNews.* http://asia.inter net.com/ 1999/2/1003-india.html (16 June 1999).

Article in a magazine on the Web
(MLA)
"Happy New Euro." *Time Daily* 30 Dec. 1998. http://cgi.pathfinder.com/time/daily/0,29 60,17455-101990101,00.html (4 Jan. 1999).
(APA)
Happy new Euro. (1998, December 30). *Time Daily.* http://cgi.pathfinder.com/time/ daily/0,2960,17455-101990101,00.html (4 Jan. 1999).

Online encyclopedia

Some encyclopedia articles have authors listed, so begin with the author's name if available. Otherwise start with the title of the entry.

(MLA)

"Semiconductor." *Encyclopaedia Britannica Online.* http://search.eb.com/bol/topic ?eu=68433&sctn=1#s_top (31 Aug. 1999).

(APA)

Semiconductor. (1999). *Encyclopaedia Britannica Online.* http://search.eb.com/ bol/topic?eu= 68433&sctn=1#s_top (31 Aug. 1999).

Graphic, audio, or video files

Graphic, audio, and video files are cited just like Web pages. Give the author's name if available, the title of the file if available, date of publication, the URL, and the date of access. If both author and title are not available, use the file name as the title.

(MLA)

"East Timor Awaits Referendum." *NPR Online* 31 Aug. 1999. http://www.npr.org/ram files/atc/19990830.atc.10.ram (31 Aug. 1999).

(APA)

East Timor awaits referendum. (1999, August 31). *NPR Online.* http://www.npr.org/ram files/atc/19990830.atc.10.ram (31 Aug. 1999).

Gopher site

Gopher is an information protocol system that stores files in directories much like your home computer. Give the author's name, the title of the page or file, date of publication, the address, and the date of access.

(MLA)

Marcos (Subcomandante Insurgente). "The Story of Durito and the Defeat of Neo-Liberalism." 15 Aug. 1995. gopher://

mundo.eco.utexas.edu:70/0R0-5940-/
mailing/chiapas95.archive/EZLN%
20Communiques/Tales%20of%20Durito
(31 Aug. 1999).

(APA)

Marcos. (1995, August 15). The story of
Durito and the defeat of neo-liberalism.
gopher://mundo.eco.utexas.edu:70/0R0
-5940-/mailing/chiapas95.archive/EZLN
%20Communiques/Tales%20of%20Durito
(31 August, 1999).

Listserv posting

Give the author's name or alias, the subject line,
date of posting, the newsgroup address, and the
date of access.

(MLA)

Selzer, Jack. "Ed Corbett." 4 July 1998.
WPA-L@lists.asu.edu (7 July 1998).

(APA)

Selzer, J. (1998, July 4). Ed Corbett.
WPA-L@lists.asu.edu (7 July 1998).

Newsgroup posting

Give the author's name or alias, the subject line,
date of posting, the newsgroup address, and the
date of access.

(MLA)

Brody, Philip. "Chamax." 9 May 1999. news:
sci.archaeology.mesoamerican (12 May
1999).

(APA)

Brody, P. (1999, May 9). Chamax. news:
sci.archaeology.mesoamerican (12 May
1999).

Personal email

Delete the email address and use "personal email"
instead. APA and other scientific styles usually omit
personal email from the list of references.

(MLA)
Wilson, Samuel. "Advantages of Flash 3."
    Personal email (18 Aug. 1999).
(APA)
Wilson, S. (1999, August 18). Advantages of
    Flash 3. [personal email].

Documenting Sources on a Web Site

Web sites provide you the opportunity to link direct-ly to other Web sites. Thus when you make a refer-ence to another Web site, you can make a link off the author's name or the title of the Web site that takes you directly to it. By clicking these links, a visitor to your site can immediately consult the source. Nonetheless, it's still a good idea to include a works-cited list. One reason is because you don't neces-sarily want your visitors leaving your site in the mid-dle of what you have to say. If you link off the works-cited list to other Web sites, the visitor will have at least had a chance to read your text first. The sec-ond reason is that it's good to have all of your refer-ences in one place. A third reason is that because Web sites change so quickly and often disappear, the date you accessed the source you cite is impor-tant. If you want to have links within your text, you might consider making them to the works-cited list rather than taking your visitors to another site.

What Else a Web Site Can Do for You

CHAPTER 10

Successful Résumés

Focus on the employer's needs

The Web can help you find a good job, but it should be only one aspect for your overall strategy. First, you should start thinking about what kind of job you would like to get long before you graduate. You may be able to arrange an internship in your chosen field while you are still in school and get paid for gaining valuable experience. When you begin the serious job search, finding the right job depends on writing a successful résumé—one of the most important pieces of writing you will ever compose. The secret of a successful résumé is understanding its purpose. Above all, the purpose of your résumé is to get interviews with potential employers. Great jobs often attract many applicants. A successful résumé will place you among the small group of candidates to be interviewed.

Begin by imagining that you are the person who will make the decision on which candidate to hire. Likely that person will be either the head of or a key member of the team that you hope to join. From that person's perspective what qualities would the ideal candidate have? What would distinguish that candidate from other well qualified candidates? Make a list of those qualities and put checks beside the ones you believe are most important. Then assess your own qualifications. What abilities and experiences do you have that match those of the ideal candidate?

Elements of a successful résumé

Many people think of a résumé as a life history beginning with elementary school. Nothing could be duller or less effective in a highly competitive job search. Instead think of your résumé as an advertisement for yourself. In a very short space, you have to convince the prospective employer that you are competent, energetic, and can get along well with coworkers. Successful résumés typically have two critical sections at the beginning: an **objective** section where you name the position you want and a **summary** section where you focus on your most important qualifications and experience.

The objective section should be targeted for the position you are applying for. The key is to be as specific as possible, using the language of the target field. Vague, empty phrases such as "Seek an entry-level position that presents new challenges and will fully utilize my talents" earns your résumé a quick trip to the rejected pile. One method is to name the position, the target location, and the two most important qualities for excelling in that position. For example:

- Credit reviewer in Central or South America where familiarity with local banking systems and fluency in Spanish and Portuguese are essential.

- Special education teacher in the greater Atlanta area specializing in brain injured patients and requiring familiarity with coordinating ARDS and completing IED documentation.
- Web developer for financial Web sites with database backend requiring complex troubleshooting and skills in HTML, JavaScript, Cold Fusion, SQL, NT. Preferred location in New England, especially Boston.

The summary section consists of short statements of the most important qualifications you bring to the position. These highlights will be closely read on the initial review. It is your opportunity to convince the employer that you are worth a closer look.

- Two years' experience analyzing computer system requirements and designing computer system specifications based on projected workloads.
- Supervised, trained and assessed the work of staff (1-4) involved in audit assists.
- Reviewed real estate investments and loan portfolios for documentation, structure, credit analysis, risk identification, and credit scoring.
- Exceptional interpersonal skills in managing a large leasing office. Created productive relationships among clients, staff, and corporate executives.

Following the summary section is where you go into more detail. This section lists your skills and accomplishments, areas of expertise, and educational background. How you structure this section depends on what you have to offer. List work experience in reverse chronological order, focusing on your more recent jobs and including details of your duties and accomplishments. Likewise, list your education in reverse chronological order, with certificates or degrees earned placed first. You can conclude by placing "References available upon request" at the end, but this line is not necessary.

Unless you are asked, do not include the actual names and addresses of your references, but instead bring them on a separate sheet to the interview.

Scannable and traditional résumés

The career center at your college is the place to start when you are looking for a job. Very likely they will have a résumé service that employers use to find promising job candidates and set up interviews. The career counselors can give you good advice about how to format your résumé and what to include in it. Most career counselors now recommend that you create two printed résumés—a scannable résumé and a traditional résumé.

A traditional résumé often has bullets, italics, boldfacing, and different type sizes. While it may look attractive, it is not well suited for human resource departments at medium and large companies, who typically scan résumés and put them in a database. Bullets, boldfacing, and fancy backgrounds can confuse scanners. The company is interested only in the text on the résumé, which is what goes into the database. The company uses the database to search for qualified applicants when new positions become available. You might wonder why you can't just send your traditional résumé as an attachment to an email message, thus avoiding the step of scanning. The reason is that many companies do not accept attachments because so many carry computer viruses.

Your scannable résumé should be clean and simple. Because your résumé is screened by a machine and not a person, your strategy changes accordingly. Your Web résumé must use words that can be scanned, sorted, and retrieved by the search engine. The employer will do keyword searches on the résumé database, so it's critical to anticipate which keywords the employer might use to find you. For example, an employer might search for "Oracle RDBMS," "database administration," and "data modeling." If you have "Oracle RDBMS" and "database administration" but not "data modeling," you could be overlooked. The strategy is to include as many different nouns as possible that might describe you.

The temptation is to dump a bunch of nouns into a paragraph at the beginning of the résumé; while this tactic might get you recognized by the search engine, it's not going to be effective when the recruiter pulls up your résumé to read. Thus you shouldn't ignore the traditional elements of a résumé, including a work history. But you should also remember that like other kinds of Web sites, what's up front is the most critical. You should have your work objective and a summary of your skills at the beginning. Other points to keep in mind are:

- Use a 10- or 12-point sans serif font—Helvetica or Arial.
- Do not underline, boldface, or use italics because these features can confuse scanners.
- Place your text flush against the left margin.
- Avoid graphics and lines because scanners do not recognize them.
- Use white space. The one design element that doesn't confuse scanners is white space.
- Know the language of the field. Read job descriptions carefully for the words used to describe particular positions.
- Emphasize your computer skills.

Putting your résumé on the Web

In addition, you might consider putting your résumé on the Web. Since there are millions of Web pages, you might ask why bother? You might think that your odds would be better nailing your résumé to a telephone pole in the hope that someone would walk by and see it. If indeed you had to depend on an employer finding your site by chance, the odds would be close to those of winning the lottery.

Fortunately, you don't have to depend on chance. You can send the URL of your résumé to email addresses or post it in a discussion group. There are also commercial job data banks where you can place your online résumé for a small fee. If you use one of these services, it is good to know in advance which employers will be sending in queries. Furthermore, if your résumé is on the Web, more and more employers are using search tools to find you. Often job ads do not attract an adequate pool of candidates. Employers also want to know who might be available for future openings.

You can use a Web translator to convert your scannable résumé to a Web page using the "Save as HTML" command. Another easy option is to copy the scannable résumé into an HTML page and insert the <PRE> tag before and the </PRE> tag after. If you also want a better looking traditional résumé on the Web, consider using a two-column table format. Divide the columns about 25% / 75%. That way you can place the descriptors in the left column (Objective, Summary, Education, and so on) and the statements that match these descriptors in the right column.

Creating Web Sites for Clubs and Organizations

Student clubs and organizations have been quick to create Web sites. Because these sites are aimed at a college audience who often prefers to get its information from the Web, it's no surprise that students in these clubs have turned to the Web to get the word out about their club or activity. At most colleges and universities you can see a list of student-run clubs and organizations in the student section of the school's Web site. From there you can click on to the sites for various clubs and organizations.

Creating community on the Web

If you check out several of the Web sites for the student clubs and organizations at your school, you can quickly spot differences. Some are like print brochures that tell you about the club and look nice but haven't been updated for a long time. Others are massive sites where you can find lots of evidence of member participation on the site—discussion lists, trip reports, photographs, schedules of upcoming events. Both kinds of sites serve particular needs, but even a quick glance will tell you that if you want a site that users will come back to frequently, you have to provide a reason for them to return.

Users who come back to a site again and again expect the content of the site to be current and the information of benefit to them. They also expect the site to create a sense of community—both on the site where members often post notices and participate in the discussion groups and off the site where members find out when and where activities and events will take place. The MIT Cycling Club, for example, posts current race results, has a schedule of rides, links to other cycling sites, forms for registering for races, and a photo gallery (see Figure 10.1).

The design process

When you design a Web site for a club or organization, you should begin by thinking through the design process described in Chapter 3.

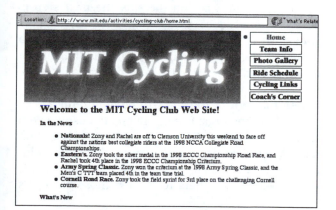

FIGURE 10.1 MIT Cycling Club home page

1. Articulate your goals

What is the club or organization's main purpose? What are the main purposes of the Web site? Do you want more members to join? Do you want to keep current members more involved? Do you want to make yourself known to similar clubs at other colleges and elsewhere?

2. Categorize your target audience

Who is the site intended for? You might list all possible audiences such as current student members, prospective student members, faculty, students at other colleges, and other interested people. How important is each? What kind of access to the Web are they likely to have?

3. Determine what content you need and how you will obtain it

What content should go on your site? Where will you find the content? How much will you depend on members to contribute content? Do you want to add interactivity with a bulletin board or a chat area? How important are links to other sites? Who has the authority to sign off on what goes on the Web site?

4. Determine the structure of your site

Deciding on the main areas of the site should be one of the first things you do. When you have a complete list of what you want on the site, the next step is deciding what goes with what. Restructuring or adding on later can be a nightmare if you have to change all the navigational tools. The handful of main topics should be reflected in your navigational tools.

5. Determine how the site will be maintained

Many clubs and organizations put up handsome Web sites only to allow them to become quickly out-of-date. All student organizations have difficulties with turnover; active members graduate and sometimes it takes a while for others to occupy those slots. It's

important to establish one or more positions responsible for maintaining and updating the site.

Making Money on the Web

Designing Web sites for others

Aside from investing in hot Internet stocks, there
are two basic ways of making money on the Web—
designing and managing Web sites for others and
establishing your own business on the Web. In the
early days of the Web, many Web savvy students
had great part-time jobs doing Web design. Today
there are no shortage of companies in the Web
design business, and many firms have their own in-
house Web design staff. Nevertheless, there are still
many opportunities to make money by designing
Web sites, but if you think you want to get into this
business in a serious way, you have to be prepared
to put in a great deal of effort.

If you do get serious, you'll want to upgrade your
skills through course work and by studying on your
own. It's a good idea to work for someone else first.
There's a lot more to designing a Web site for pay
than just the technical side. You need to know how
to determine pricing, negotiate with the client, set a
schedule, develop a plan for maintenance, and many
other aspects. You have to be able to size up clients
at the beginning, and recognize those who will make
decisions by committee and are likely to want many
changes before they accept your work. Your people
skills may be as important as your Web skills.

Running your own Web business

The other primary way to make money on the Web
is to run your own business using the Web as a mar-
keting and sales tool. You may have a great idea for
a Web business, but you might also think that you
have little chance for success given that there are

millions of other Web sites and the big players have the big advertising budgets to get Web surfers to their sites.

Before you give up too quickly, remember that the Web is a very different medium from anything that has come before. You can put up a great deal of information including color photographs and even video quite cheaply. Best of all, you can make your site visible to search engines, so if a user is looking for a specific kind of product or service, the right words on your site will enable that user to find you. Don't expect to get rich overnight from your online business, but if you enjoy designing Web pages, you can earn some income from your interests.

Niche marketing

The Web allows people with highly specialized interests to find each other if they can connect through precise keywords. For example, if your hobby is collecting, it's not hard to locate other collectors. Yahoo lists over 1200 sites on collectibles—probably a small fraction of the number out there (see Figure 10.2).

There are many great possibilities besides collectibles that take only your time and the investment of space on a Web server to get started. For example, one student worked for a company that installed lawn sprinklers. He realized that many people could install their own sprinkler systems if they had a plan and knew where to buy the parts. He set up a Web site that explains how easy it is to install a sprinkler system. For a fee he offers to draw a custom plan for a yard system and make a list of the parts required, including where they can be purchased. It has turned out to be a profitable part-time job with a flexible schedule.

Getting people to your site

Besides having a great business idea, you need to figure out how to get people to your site. The big players can afford expensive banner ads on major

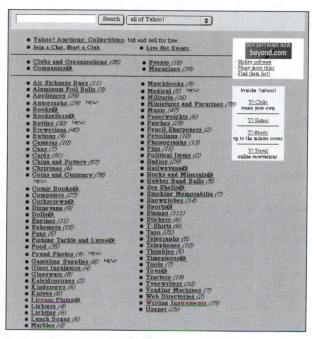

FIGURE 10.2   Yahoo collectibles list

sites and can list their URLs in print and television
advertising. You have to use other means to get
users to your site. First, take advantage of any word-
of-mouth opportunities. Sometimes you can get
other people to place links to your site on their
pages. There are some places to put free ads on the
Web, and some discussion groups that discourage
direct advertising will allow you to at least mention
the URL of your business site in a message.

Second, put META description and keywords tags
in the head section of your main page. The description text will show up verbatim in an AltaVista
search. Search engines use keywords to categorize
your site. You can list as many keywords as you can
think of that might bring up your page on a search
engine. These keywords are especially important if
your site contains mostly graphics. META tags are
easy to insert into your source file:

```
<META NAME="description"
CONTENT="Everything you need to know for
installing your own lawn sprinkler system.">
<META NAME="keywords" CONTENT="sprinkler,
lawnsprinkler, in-ground sprinkler, under-
ground sprinkler, pop-up sprinkler, irrigation,
sprinkler installation, sprinkler diagram,
sprinkler specifications">
```

Third, submit your site to Web directories. Unlike search engines that use robots or "spiders" to index Web pages, Web directories use people for this task—either professional editors or voluntary submissions. You can submit your site to Yahoo, for example. Not all sites are accepted and it may take months before your site is listed, but the effort is well worth it if you make the Yahoo directory. If you want the widest possible visibility, submit your site to all major search engines and all directories. Each includes directions on how to submit your site. There are auto-submit programs (for example, SubmitIT at www.submitit.com) that will do it for you, but you will get better results doing it yourself.

Glossary

APPENDIX A

A

absolute link Full URL address.

ActiveX Microsoft Web technology that allows software components to interact.

ADSL Asynchronous Digital Subscriber Line. High-speed connection to the Web via telephone lines.

AIFF (.aif) Audio Interchange File Format, a cross-platform format for digital audio files that is commonly used on Macintoshes.

AltaVista Internet portal with powerful search engine at:
http://www.altavista.com

analog General term in electronics for signals that vary continuously across a range. Telephones, cassette recorders, radio, and television all have relied on analog signals that are being replaced by **digital** signals.

animated GIF Graphic file in GIF89a format with multiple frames that can be displayed in succession to produce most of the small animations you see on the Web.

applet A small Java program that is transmitted to computers via the Web.

ASCII American Standard Code for Information Interchange. The "plain" text format that all computers can read.

AVI Audio-Video Interleave. Windows format for video files.

B

backbone The major trunk lines that carry Internet traffic.

bandwidth The speed at which data can be transmitted, usually listed in bits per second (bps). The bigger the pipe, the faster the flow. Standard telephone modems run at 28,800 bps (28.8 kbps) or 56 kbps (although phone lines often limit the speed). Cable modems offer rates up to 10 mbps (10,000,000 bps).

baud rate The rate at which a modem's signal changes per second in transmitting data.

bit The smallest unit of digital data expressed as a binary value, either 1 or 0.

bookmarks Netscape file that stores URLs so you can return easily to pages on the Web. Called "favorites" on Internet Explorer.

browser The computer program that gives you access to the Web. Netscape and Internet Explorer are the most popular.

browser-safe colors See "Web-safe colors."

C

cable modem High-speed modem that uses cable TV lines for Internet connections.

cache Temporary storage of Web files that allows your browser to reload pages much faster.

CGI Common Gateway Interface. A combination of a Web server and external programming scripts that create Web pages.

compression Method of reducing the amount of data necessary for recreating a file, thus making the file load faster.

cookie Small file placed on your computer by the Web server so that it "recognizes" you the next time you access the site from the same browser.

CSS Cascading style sheets. See "style sheets."

D

dial-up modem Older, slower modems that use phone lines to connect with the Internet.

digital Binary coding of data into bits, either 1 or 0.

dpi Dots per inch. Measurement in print graphics for the resolution of an image.

Dynamic HTML (DHTML) A mixture of HTML, style sheets, and scripting.

E

Excite Web portal with search engine at: http://www.excite.com

F

favorites Internet Explorer file that stores URLs. Called "bookmarks" on Netscape.

fonts Typeface styles.

forms Forms enable users to enter information on a Web page by a combination of HTML and CGI.

frames Frames divide a Web page into multiple windows, with each window acting as a nested Web page.

ftp File transfer protocol. Programs that allow you to access a computer at remote locations and move files between that computer and your computer.

G

GIF Graphic Interchange Format. Preferred Web format for images with sharp lines, text, and small file sizes.

gopher An information protocol system developed at the University of Minnesota that stores files in directories.

H

home page Home page has two meanings: 1) the opening page on the user's browser; 2) the opening or main page on a Web site.

HTML HyperText Markup Language. Display language used for creating Web pages.

hypertext Document that allows users to connect to other pages or documents by clicking on links. The Web can be thought of as one huge hypertext.

I

image editors Programs that allow users to create and manipulate images.

image map An image that has been divided into regions and connected to actions, which are usually links. When you click on a particular part of the image, you jump to another Web page.

internal modem A modem that is built into your computer.

ISP Internet Service Provider. Companies such as AOL which offer Internet service.

J

Java Cross-platform programming language developed by Sun Microsystems used to create applets.

Javascript Scripting language developed by Netscape that extends the capabilities of HTML.

JPEG Joint Photographic Experts Group. Preferred Web format for photographs.

K

kbps Kilobits (1,000 bits) per second. Most dial-up telephone modems run at 28.8 kbps or 56 kbps.

L

link Words or images that connect to another Web page or file that can be displayed or downloaded.

M

mbps Megabits (1,000,000 bits) per second. Cable modems run up to 10 mbps.

meta tags Special tags that go into the header of a Web page and contain keywords. They do not appear on the screen but allow search engines to match keywords.

MIDI Musical Instrument Digital Interface. Files designed to allow computers to communicate with synthesizers, keyboards, and other digital instruments.

MP3 Mpeg-Layer III file. Files that produce high-quality recordings using relatively little space.

MPEG Compressed video and audio file format, named for the Motion Picture Experts Group of the International Standards Organization.

N

navigation bar A set of links on a Web page displayed as icons, text, or both, most often on the top of a page.

newsgroups Usenet discussion groups that allow users to post messages that all can read.

O

operating system The system software that controls a computer such as Windows, Mac OS, and UNIX.

P

PDF Portable Document Format, created by Adobe Systems for use on Adobe's Acrobat Reader.

pixel A dot on a picture that is the basic unit of images. Images are sized in pixels according to height and width.

Perl Programming language commonly used to create CGI scripts.

platform Computer hardware and operating system combination such as "Wintel," an Intel-based PC running Windows.

plug-in Helper applications that give your browser additional capabilities such as viewing QuickTime movies.

Q

QuickTime Digital video format developed by Apple which is supported on both Windows and Macintosh platforms.

R

RAM Random Access Memory. The active area of a computer's memory used for running programs.

RealMedia Popular software for streaming audio and video.

relative link Partial URL for a link to a file on the same Web site.

S

script A list of instructions that are interpreted line by line rather than compiled like programming language. Scripts are easier to read and change than programs.

search engine A program that searches information in electronic formats. Web search engines like Northern Lights and AltaVista search through indexes of the entire Web.

server Host computer for Web files.

Shockwave Multimedia player plug-in developed by Macromedia for displaying files created in Macromedia's authoring programs including Director, Flash, and Freehand.

source The HTML file that creates a Web page.

streaming audio and video Allows users to hear audio and watch video as a file is being downloaded.

style sheet A set of specifications that controls the display of a page. Style sheets can be written by either the author of a Web page or the user of the page.

T

tags HTML commands enclosed in angle brackets such as <P>.

TCP/IP Transfer Control Protocol/Internet Protocols. The protocols that allow computers to communicate on the Internet.

transparent GIF GIF image in which the background color is declared transparent, allowing the image to appear to float on a Web page.

U

UNIX Operating system used by many Web servers.

URL Universal Resource Locator. Addresses on the Web.

Usenet Collection of networks that host online discussion groups.

W

WAVE (.wav) Format for audio files that is commonly used on Windows.

Web editors Programs that allow you to compose Web pages.

Web translators Programs such as Microsoft Word and Excel that include a "Save as HTML" command.

Web-safe colors Palette of 216 colors that will appear the same on different platforms and most browsers. Also called "browser-safe colors" and "browser-safe palette."

World Wide Web Consortium (W3C) A group of representatives from universities, Web designers, and software companies who oversee the development of standards and technologies for the Web.

X, Y, Z

XML Extensible Markup Language, an alternative display language to HTML that is especially useful for defining formats for data.

Yahoo Popular Web directory at: http://www.yahoo.com

zip Compression format used for transferring and storing files.

HTML
Tags

Many people still hand code HTML with NotePad (Windows), SimpleText (Macintosh), or their word processing program using the **Save As: Text Only** command when they save the file. Even if you use a Web page editor, sometimes you may want to edit the HTML file. For the latest official information on HTML tags, consult the World Wide Web Consortium site (http://www.w3.org/Mark Up/).

The Essentials

HTML

The first and last tags on an HTML document.

```
<HTML>
</HTML>
```

Head and title

Inside the HEAD, you should put the TITLE tags and the page title between them, which will appear at the top of the browser window.

```
<HEAD>
<TITLE>your page title</TITLE>
</HEAD>
```

Body

After the HEAD section comes the BODY section. All that will be displayed on the Web page is placed between this pair of tags.

```
<BODY>
</BODY>
```

Structural Tags

Headings

For section titles use the heading tags. <H1> is the tag for the most important heading; <H6> is the tag for the least important heading.

```
<H1>Heading 1</H1>
<H2>Heading 2</H2>
<H3>Heading 3</H3>
<H4>Heading 4</H4>
<H5>Heading 5</H5>
<H6>Heading 6</H6>
```

Paragraphs and line breaks

To format paragraphs you must use the <P> tag. The closing </P> tag is optional. To start a new line without making a new paragraph, use the <BR> tag.

Horizontal rules

The <HR> tag draws a line across the text, which is often useful for separating sections. You can specify in pixels the thickness <HR SIZE=?> and width <HR WIDTH=?> of the horizontal rule.

Blockquote

The BLOCKQUOTE tag sets off and indents long quotations.

```
<BLOCKQUOTE> </BLOCKQUOTE>
```

Lists

Bullet lists

Bullet lists are called unordered lists. They begin and end with the <UL> tags, and each item is marked with the <LI> tag.

<UL>
<LI>Item 1
<LI>Item 2
<LI>Item 3
<LI>Item 4
</UL>

Numbered lists

Numbered lists are called ordered lists. They begin and end with the <OL> tags, and each item is marked with the <LI> tag.

<OL>
<LI>Item 1
<LI>Item 2
<LI>Item 3
<LI>Item 4
</OL>

Definition lists

Definition lists allow you to make a list of terms and their definitions. They begin and end with <DL> tags. Each item is marked with a <DT> tag and each definition with a <DD> tag.

<DL>
<DT>Item 1
<DD>Item 1 definition
<DT>Item 2
<DD>Item 2 definition
</DL>

Logical Style Tags

The recommended way to highlight text is to use logical tags which allow the user to specify how the tag will be displayed.

Emphasis

Emphasis usually displays as italics.
<EM></EM>

Strong emphasis

Strong emphasis usually displays as boldface.
<STRONG></STRONG>

Citation

Citation tags are used for book titles, movie titles, and other references. They usually display as italics.
<CITE></CITE>

Forced Style Tags

Forced style tags declare the appearance of text. While they run contrary to the HTML philosophy of allowing users to decide how they want text to be displayed, they are used much more frequently than logical style tags.

Boldface	<B></B>
Italics	<I></I>
Underline	<U></U>
Subscript	
Superscript	
Typewriter Text	<TT></TT>
Center	<CENTER></CENTER>
Blinking	<BLINK></BLINK>
Font Size	<FONT SIZE=3></FONT>
	(ranges from 1-7)

| Font Color | <FONT COLOR="#color number"></FONT> |
| Select Font | <FONT FACE="name of font"></FONT> |

Links

HREF

The basic structure of a link to another file or Web page is <A HREF="URL">linked text</A>.

Linking within a document

Suppose your document is long and you want to allow users to go back to the top at frequent intervals. First insert a named anchor in the HTML file using the form <A NAME="top">anchor text</A>. The anchor text does not show up as a link but is simply a named location where you can send users. Next insert links later in your document. You might insert "Back to top" in your text with this command: <A HREF="#top">Back to top</A>. The pound sign (#) tells the browser to look for the named anchor "top."

Linking to anchors on other pages

You also can make links to specific places on other pages if you insert named anchors. Suppose you have a table of contents file for a long document and you want to enable users to go directly to particular parts. If you have inserted the anchors "part1," "part2," and so on at the appropriate places in the file document.html, then you can use this command: <A HREF="document.html#part2"></A>.

Link to email

You can make it easy for users to email you with this command:
<A HREF="mailto:wonderfulme@aol.com">Send me mail</A>

Images

Adding images

The width and height specifications in pixels are not necessary but they make the page load faster. For example:

`<IMG SRC="whale.jpg" WIDTH=295 HEIGHT=195>`

Aligning images

You can declare where you want the image to appear on the page. For example:

`<IMG SRC="URL"`
`ALIGN=TOP|BOTTOM|MIDDLE|LEFT|RIGHT>`

Alt attribute

The ALT attribute gives a short description that will display for users who choose not to load images or cannot see them, as in:

`<IMG SRC="whale.jpg" WIDTH=295 HEIGHT=195`
`ALT="picture of humpback whale breaching">`

Backgrounds and Colors

You can find color numbers at many locations on the Web, such as the Color Picker tool at http://junior .apk.net/~jbarta/tutor/makapage/picker/index.html, which is available for download in zip format.

Background image	`<BODY BACKGROUND="URL">`
Background color	`<BODY BGCOLOR="# color number">`
Text color	`<BODY TEXT="#color number">`
Link color	`<BODY LINK ="#color number">`
Visited link	`<BODY VLINK ="#color number">`

Active link   <BODY ALINK ="#color
                               number">

Tables

Tables are defined with a pair of tags: <TABLE>
</TABLE>. Rows are defined with the TR tag and
cells with the TD tag. Other tags are explained in a
tables tutorial at http://junior.apk.net/~jbarta/tutor/
tables/index.html. The table below is produced by
the HTML code that follows:

Column 1	Column 2
Item 1A	Item 2A
Item 1B	Item 2B

```
<TABLE BORDER COLS=2 WIDTH="50%" BORDER=1>
<TR>
<TD><B>Column 1</B></TD>
<TD><B>Column 2</B></TD>
</TR>
<TR>
<TD>Item 1A</TD>
<TD>Item 2A</TD>
</TR>
<TR>
<TD>Item 1B</TD>
<TD>Item 2B</TD>
</TR>
</TABLE>
```

Special Characters

Refer to http://www.w3.org/TR/REC-html/sgml/
entities.html for a complete list of special characters. Remember, special characters must be in lower
case.

Character name	Character	HTML tag
Nonbreaking space		
Less than	<	&lt;
Greater than	>	&gt;
Ampersand	&	&amp;
Quotation mark	"	&quot;
Copyright	©	&copy;
Registered	®	&reg;
Cent	¢	&cent;
British pound	£	&pound;
Yen	¥	&yen;
Degree	°	&deg;
Plus-or-minus sign	±	&plusmn;
Division sign	÷	&divide;
Paragraph	¶	&para;
Inverted question mark	¿	&iquest;
Inverted exclamation	¡	&iexcl;

Index